COMPACT CYMRU

Welsh Poetry:

Music and Metres

Selected and translated by Howard Huws

Gwasg Carreg Gwalch

First published in 2017

© images: Gwasg Carreg Gwalch and Crown
copyright (2016) Visit Wales
Marian Delyth © page 32
Keith O'Brien © pages 43, 84, 104

© publication: Gwasg Carreg Gwalch 2017

ISBN: 978-1-84524-250-3

Cover design: Eleri Owen
Cover image: Keith O'Brien

Published with the financial support
of the Welsh Books Council

Published by Gwasg Carreg Gwalch,
12 Iard yr Orsaf, Llanrwst, Wales LL26 0EH
tel: 01492 642031
email: llanrwst@carreg-gwalch.com
website: www.carreg-gwalch.com

Acknowledgements

We wish to thank the following writers, publishers
and other owners of copyright for granting
permission for the poems which are included in this
book.

Gwasg Gomer
Jennifer Thomas
Mirain Llwyd Owen
Nia Llwyd
Emyr Lewis
Idris Reynolds
Ifor ap Glyn
Mari George
Rhys Iorwerth
Catrin Dafydd
Gruffudd Antur

Every effort has been made to contact the owners of
copyright, but this has not always proved possible.
We therefore offer our apologies to any publishers,
agencies or individuals who have been omitted from
the above list. If they would like to contact the
publisher this will ensure that their names are
included in the event of the book being reprinted.

*Page 1: Dafydd ap Gwilym was one of the
most important medieval poets in Europe –
this gravestone is under the yew tree at the
abbey of Ystrad Fflur, Ceredigion*

Contents

Foreword

Academics tell us that modern Welsh verse includes craft elements which derive from the oral poetry of the ancestral Celts, 3,500 years ago: yet these, together with metre and verse patterns developed in medieval courts and taverns, are still in use. Poetry is still an essential, vigorous and very popular part of contemporary Welsh culture, giving colour to national and everyday life.

From early sixth century heroic odes to the young voices of the twenty-first century, this collection offers an insight into a special tradition. Professor Peredur Lynch of Bangor University has shown that the Welsh, along with the Zulu nation in South Africa, are rare examples of societies managing to adapt the traditional praise poetry of their old professional poets to the needs of the present day. They have succeeded in doing this whilst, at the same time, keeping and developing their audiences.

The oral origins, and indeed the social nature of modern Welsh poetry, give much attention to word music craft, threaded and woven together to create 'strict metre verse'. Each line of each metre (and there are twenty four and more different traditional metres, as well as new ones being experimented with constantly) is constructed according to *cynghanedd*, a term best (but not precisely) translated as 'harmony'. Though it goes back to the mists of early civilization, it remains a poetic force to this day. The effect of hearing *cynghanedd* poetry read out loud, or sung to the harp, can be arousing: but it is not all about the pleasures of the senses. It also lifts and carries, and at its greatest, can bear the burdens of an entire people.

Safeguarding Welshness – from investing in archaeology to creating new laws; from reviving the language to defending land ownership; from protecting heritage and environment to promoting Welsh produce – has been a primary theme in Welsh politics and culture over the last half century. Safeguarding a poetic tradition means using it: singing new verse in it, finding a new audience for it, and maintaining active links with the Welsh language rock and pop scene. Drawing strength from its long roots, Welsh poetry and the new revival in *cynghanedd* celebrates the rebirth of the nation.

If the term for this poetry itself is untranslatable, how did Howard Huws find himself with the task of trying to convey the music and meaning of Welsh verse in another language? Literal word-for-word translation would be possible, but pedestrian: he has to respect the effects of the vowels, the consonants and the accents on the ear. A poet chooses his words carefully: he may have a choice of six different possible words to end a certain line – each one offers subtly different meanings and allusions, as well as different acoustic combinations.

Howard, similarly, has to choose. He likens the process of translating poetry to a crossword puzzle, in which the answers to one set of clues have to be changed into a different language, but must still provide the same answers, in the same spaces, at the same intersections, losing none of their force and meaning. He has to capture the power of the original verse, including the rhythmic body attack of a simple line of words. What we have here is a Welsh adventure into the English language.

Poetry is more than a literary form. It is a vessel which contains a people's response to the land in which they live, and the history of their experiences. Landscapes and locations in time are reflected in the lines. Images of Wales, by some of the country's best photographers, sit well beside these poems.

Myrddin ap Dafydd

The Age of Heroes

A thick, dark mist envelops us: so thick as to deaden all sound. Then a gust swirls it aside, and suddenly we find ourselves in the din and confusion of a battlefield, where screaming warriors are hacking and stabbing at each other, champions on horseback bark out challenges, and the wounded stagger in bloodied rivers like drunkards in pools of wine. We glance upwards, and see crows and eagles wheeling high above, waiting to descend and tear at the flesh of the dead. They'll soon get their chance.

That night, birds and men alike are feasting. We're in a crowded hall, brightly lit, where there's meat and mead and wine and singing. Then quiet, as a poem is recited, recalling the chieftain's descent from ancient heroes, and declaiming to all present how worthy a successor, how ferocious a warrior, how generous a provider is he who gained victory today. At some time in future, a poet will compose the same chieftain's elegy, mourning his loss and encouraging his successors to emulate him: or if things go badly, may lament the destruction of all that has gone before, picturing the hall as ruined and desolate.

Such is our introduction to the earliest Welsh poetry. It's the poetry of an heroic society, ruled by kings whose status rests on their ancestry, their ability as fighters, and their generosity towards dependents. The setting isn't present-day Wales, but the Welsh-speaking lands from the midland valley of Scotland down into Yorkshire and Cumbria, as far as Cheshire and Shropshire: known in Welsh as *Yr Hen Ogledd*, the 'Old North' of the sixth and seventh centuries AD. Though they owe much to their Celtic ancestors, these people are Christians, think of themselves as civilized Romans (still in contact with the remains of the Empire), and are well aware of Classical literature.

In this culture, poets are afforded high status, and are expected to compose verse proclaiming and reinforcing society's values. They're propagandists, entertainers, psychologists, seers, chroniclers, and warriors in their own

'Gwŷr a aeth Gatraeth...'
The heroic poetry about the Battle of Catterick in the Book of Aneirin

cattau · a gwedy chwed rawelwch vu · ker elwynt e lanneu
e benydu · dadyl dieu aghen y eu treidu ·

Gwyr a aeth gatraeth veduaeth uedron · ffyryf frwythlawn oed cam nas kymhwyllwn · e am lavnawr coch gor
vawr gwrmwn · dwys dengyn ed emledyn aergwn · ar
deulu brenneych beych barnasswn · dihyw dyn en vyw nys
adawsswn · kyueillt a golleis diffleis oedwn · rugyl en em
wrthryn ryvm riadwn · ny mennws gwrawl gwadawl
chwegrwn · maban y gian o vaen gwynngwn ·

Gwyr a aeth gatraeth gan wawr trauodynt eu bed
eu hoynawr · milcant a thrychant a emdaflawr · gwyar
llyt gwynnodynt waewawr · ef gorsaf yng gwryaf eg
gwryawr · rac gosgord mynydawc mwynvawr ·

Gwyr a aeth gatraeth gan wawr dygymyrrwys eu ho
et eu hanyanawr · med evynt melyn melys maglawr blwy
ydyn bu llewyn llawer kerdawr · coch eu dedyuawr na
phurawr eu llain · gwyngalch a phedryollt beunawr rac
gosgord mynydawc mwynvawr ·

right. To sponsor a poet, or receive favourable mention in his compositions, brings great prestige: but get on the wrong side of him, and he'll respond with a crushing public put-down, bringing disgrace and even physical illness to the offender.

It's an oral culture, where people make full use of the considerable powers of human memory to compose, remember and transmit poems long and short. A few clerics can read and write, and the written word is regarded with awe. Writing – *scripture* – is reserved for only the most important matters, such as religion. At some point, however, men will see fit to expand the canon of 'scripture' to include exalted and significant poetry of the past, so as to give meaning and purpose to the present, and hope for the future.

So eventually the deeds and character of the brave men of old will be preserved and transmitted not only by memory, but also in manuscript: and along with the praise and lament, copyists will accidentally slip marginal doodles in among the other verses. A lullaby; a comment on an event, or a reflection on nature. Small, rare glimpses of a rich but otherwise unrecorded tradition of 'everyday' verse, unconcerned with heroic feats, but existing alongside the epics all the time.

What may have gone before our earliest known poetry remains unknown: but when we first encounter Welsh verse, it already has features which will distinguish it down the coming centuries. Technically, it makes use of metre and rhythm, external and internal rhyme, assonance and alliteration. This means that the poet has to be as much a musician as a wordsmith: for to compose to best effect he must have an ear to the sounds his words make. He sets up a rhythm; counts syllables; feels for the accents and stresses in the line; balances consonants tautly, but leaves just enough slack to carry the narrative from one rhyme to the next, and on to a conclusion.

Superficially, this looks like pointless constraint: and so it is, to the unskilled. But in the gifted, this discipline nurtures such formidable powers of expression as to render their poetry beautiful, precise and unforgettable. A Welsh ode is the aural equivalent of the Book of Kells: colourful, interwoven, invoking. It's as if Celts can't leave a straight line alone: it must be transfigured into a work of art which opens the mind to the unimagined.

Earlier Welsh poetry, located outside the border of modern day Wales, is dated between c. 600 AD and 850 AD, but scholars who have studied the wordcraft suggest that there was already a 2,000 year old tradition behind such mastery of verse.

Our earliest poetry is also a social one. Accomplished or not, the poet isn't a cloistered academic, divorced from others. He's a member of the community, and firmly one with them. They're his inspiration and audience. He celebrates, laments, praises and comments within that society where he learnt his craft, and to whose younger members he will transmit it in turn. So it remains: and I can think of few other cultures in this world where the same could still be said to be true. Zulu praise poetry would be one such.

Another early and lasting feature of the poetry is a strong and precise sense of place. Events don't happen in a woolly 'somewhere' far away and long ago: they happened here, in this spot. No, not *there*: **here**, in this fortress, this ford, this field.

It's a poetic key to the physical landscape, which can be read like Braille, and in which hills and hollows have their own stories and significance, to those who can recall the verses. Again, who else still does this? Native peoples of Australia come to mind, as they conjure and describe the events of Dreamtime.

Redyf gwr oed

gwas gwrhyt un das. meirch marth myngvras.

a dan vordwyt megyr... ysgwyt ysgaun lledan

ar bedrein mein vuan. kledyuawr glas glan edyf eur

aphan ny bi ef a vi cas e rof a thi. gwell gwneif a thi

ar wawr dy uoli. kynt y waet e lawr nogyr y neithya

... kynt y vwyt y vrein noc y argyurein. ... kyueillt

... ewein. kwl y uot adan vrein. marth ym py vri llad

yn mab marro.

... kynhorawc men ... diffun ymlaen

... med a dalher. twll tal y rodawr ene klywei awr yn

... rodet nawd meint. dilynei ny dylyei o gamhawn eny

verei waet mal brwyn gomynei gwyr nyt echer. pyf

... adrawd gododin ar llawr mordei. rac pebyll madawc

pan ... namen un gwr o gant eny delhei.

... kynnryfyat kynylvar e rwyf ruthyr eryr en

... pan ... e auyr a vu nor a garwsi gwell

... wnaeth e aruaeth ny gilywyst. rac bedin ododin ode

... hyder gymhell ar wyrhel ...

Owain

Gredyf gwr oed gwas
Gwrhyt am dias
Meirch mwth myngvras
A dan vordwyt megyrwas
Ysgwyt ysgauyn lledan
Ar bedrein mein vuan
Kledyuawr glas glan
Ethy eur aphan
Ny bi ef a vi
Cas e rof a thi
Gwell gwneif a thi
Ar wawt dy uoli
Kynt y waet elawr
Nogyt y neithyawr
Kynt y vwyt y vrein
Noc y argyurein
Ku kyueillt ewein
Kwl y uot a dan vrein
Marth ym pa vro
Llad un mab marro

Owain
Aneirin, 6th century

Boy in age, man by nature,
Valiant in slaughter,
Swift steeds under
His thigh, fair rider;
A wide shield over
His horse's crupper,
Clean, blue blade wielder,
Belt gold and silver.
Never could we
Be at enmity:
In song I praise you,
As is your due.
Sooner his blood spilling,
Than he to his wedding;
Sooner becoming
Crows' food than going
To the ritual
Of his own funeral.
Owain, friend most loved,
Now in crows covered.
Terrible to me
The place where he
Was slain, Marro's son,
His only one.

Stafell Gynddylan (*detholiad*)

Stauell gyndylan ys tywyll heno,
heb dan, heb wely.
Wylaf wers; tawaf wedy.

Stauell gyndylan ys tywyll heno,
heb dan, heb gannwyll.
Namyn duw, pwy a'm dyry pwyll?

Stauell gyndylan ys tywyll heno,
heb dan, heb oleuat.
E[t]lit a'm daw amdanat.

Stauell gyndylan ys tywyll y nenn,
gwedy gwen gyweithyd.
Gwae ny wna da a'e dyuyd.

Stauell gyndylan ys digarat heno,
gwedy yr neb pieuat.
Wi a angheu, byr y'm gat?

Stauell gyndylan, nyt esmwyth heno,
ar benn carrec hytwyth,
heb ner, heb niuer, heb amwyth.

Cynddylan's Hall (*selection*)
Attrib. Heledd
6th century, probably composed 9th century

Cynddylan's hall is dark tonight,
There's no bed, no firelight;
I'll weep awhile, then be quiet.

Cynddylan's hall is dark tonight,
There's no fire, no candlelight;
Who but God keeps my mind aright?

Cynddylan's hall is dark tonight,
Bereft of fire, of any light;
With longing for you, I'm beset.

Cynddylan's hall, black your roof-tree
After the fair company;
Sad that no good came to thee.

Cynddylan's hall lies deserted – tonight,
With its owner departed;
Oh Death, why leave me behind?

Cynddylan's hall, all comfortless – tonight
On its rocky fastness;
No lord, no hosts: defenceless.

Eryr Pengwern

Eryr Pengwern pengarn llwyd, heno
Aruchel ei adlais,
Eiddig am gig a gerais.

Eryr Pengwern pengarn llwyd, heno
Aruchel ei eban,
Eiddig am gig Cynddylan.

Eryr Pengwern pengarn llwyd, heno
Aruchel ei adaf,
Eiddig am gig a garaf.

Eryr Pengwern, pell galwawd heno,
Ar waed gwyr gwylawd;
Rhy elwir Tren tref ddiffawd.

Eryr Pengwern, pell gelwid heno
Ar waed gwyr gwylid;
Rhy elwir Tren tref lethrid.

The eagle of Pengwern
Attrib. Heledd
6th century, probably composed 9th century

Eagle of Pengwern, grey-maned – tonight
How loud his calling!
My loved one's flesh craving.

Eagle of Pengwern, grey-maned – tonight
How loud his screeching!
Cynddylan's flesh craving.

Eagle of Pengwern, grey-maned – tonight
How eager his clawing!
My beloved's flesh craving.

Eagle of Pengwern, long he calls – tonight
On men's blood looking;
Trenn's luck will be called lacking.

Eagle of Pengwern, long he calls – tonight
On men's blood feasting;
Trenn was said to be shining.

Marwnad Gwên (detholiad)

Gwen wrth Lawen yd welas neithwyr,
[Cat g]athuc ny techas,
Oer adrawd, ar glawd gorlas,

Gwen wrth Lawen yd wylwys neithwyr
A'r ysgwyt ar y ysgwyd.
Kan bu mab ymi bu hywyd.

Gwen wrth Lawen yd wyliis neithwyr
A'r ysgwyt ar y guis.
Kan bu mab ymi ny egis,

Gwen vordwyt tylluras. a wylyas neithwyr,
Ygoror Ryt Uorlas.
Kan bu mab ymi ny thechas.

Gwen, gwydwn dy eissillut.
Ruth [yr] eryr yn ebyr oedut.
Betwn dedwyd dianghut.

Tonn tyruit; toit eruit.
Pan aut ky[v]rein ygovit,
Gwen, gwae rhyen o'th etlit.

*Rhyd Forlas – the ford on the stream
between Shropshire and Wales. It marked a
frontier in the sixth century as it does today.*

The elegy of Gwên (selection)
Attrib. Llywarch Hen
6th century, probably composed 9th century

Gwên by the Llawen, last night – kept watch,
And he yielded nought;
At the Ford of Morlas, sad report.

Gwên by the Llawen, last night – kept watch,
Shield on shoulder aright;
As he was my son, he was fleet.

Gwên by the Llawen, last night – kept watch,
Shield to lips, he fought;
He was my son: not put to flight.

Gwên, strong of thigh, last night – kept watch,
At the Ford of Morlas about;
He was my son: he'd not retreat.

Gwên, I knew you as a battler,
A sea-eagle, rushing striker;
You'd have escaped, were I luckier.

Loud the wave that comes covering – the shore
At the warriors' mustering;
Woe, Gwên, the old man for your missing.

Oed gwr vy mab, oed [d]is[y]wen hawl,
Ac oed nei y Vryen,
Ar Ryt Vorlas y llas Gwen.

Pedwarmeib ar hugeint a'm bu,
Eurdorchawc tywyssawc llu.
Oed Gwen goreu onadu.

Pedwarmeib ar hugeint a'm bwyat,
Eurdorchawc tywyssawc cat.
Oed Gwen goreu mab o'e dat.

Pedwarmeib ar hugeint a'm bwyn.
Eurdorchawc tywyssawc vnbynn.
Wrth Wen gweissyonein oedyn,

Pedwarmeib ar hugeint yg kenueint Lywarch.
O wyr glew galwytheint.
Twll eudyot clot trameint,

Pedwarmeib ar hugeint a ueithyeint vygknawt
Drwy vyn tauawt lledesseint.
Da dyuot vygcot colledeint.

My son, man among men – tenacious
And nephew to Urien;
At the Ford of Morlas died Gwên.

I had sons four and twenty
Gold-torqued among hosts, and princely;
Gwên was dearest to me.

I had sons four and twenty
Gold-torqued in battle, and princely;
Gwên, father's favourite was he.

I had sons four and twenty
Gold-torqued princes, but only
Boys beside Gwên, so manly.

Llywarch's host, four and twenty – fierce sons,
Who fought so bravely;
Too much praise: it ends badly.

Four and twenty sons begotten – of my flesh
And by my tongue fallen;
Better scant praise. They're all gone.

Mathrafal – the motte marks the medieval court of the princes of Powys near Meifod. The poetic tradition followed its migration from Pengwern to Mathrafal.

Englynion y beddau *(detholiad)*

Y beddau a'u tud gwyddwal –
ni llesaint heb ymddial:
Gwrien, Morien, a Morial.

Bedd Tydai Tad Awen
Yng ngodir Bryn Aren.
Yn ydd wna ton tolo –
bedd Dylan Llanfeuno.

Bedd Seithennin synnwyr fan
i rwng Caer Genedr a glan
môr, mawrhydig a gynran.

Yn Aber Gwenoli,
Y mae bedd Pryderi.
Yn y tery tonnau tir
Yng Ngarrog – bedd Gwallog Hir.

The graves *(selection)*
Anonymous
8th – 9th century

The graves by the thickets hidden,
Morial, Morien and Gwrien:
slain but avenged were these men.

The grave of Tydai, Great Poet,
in Bryn Aren's lowland yet.
By the nosy breakers, so
Dylan's grave at Llanfeuno.

Seithennyn most wise in lore,
his grave's between the sea shore
and Caer Genedr: no chief more.

At Aber Gwenoli,
the grave of Pryderi.
Where the waves of Carrog fall,
there's a grave: Gwallog the Tall.

Maen Dylan, Aberdesach near Clynnog Fawr:
'Dylan's grave at Llanfeuno'

Bedd mab Osfran yng Nghamlan
gwedi llawer cyflafan.
Bedd Bedwyr yn allt Tryfan.

Bedd i Farch, bedd i Wythur,
Bedd i Wgon Gleddyfrudd.
Anoeth byd, bedd i Arthur.

Y tri bedd yng Nghefn Celfi,
awen a'u dywod imi –
bedd Cynon, garw ei ddwyael,
bedd Cynfal, bedd Cynfeli.

Bedd Gwell yn y Rhiw Felen.
Bedd Sawyl yn Llangollen.
Gwarcheidw Llam y Bwlch Llorien.

Bedd Gwaeanwyn, gŵr gofri,
Y rhwng Llifon a Llyfni.
Gŵr oedd ef gwir i neb ni roddi.

After much fighting, Osfran's
son is buried at Camlan.
Bedwyr's grave is on Tryfan.

A grave for March, a grave for Gwythur,
a grave for Gwgon Red-sword: harder
to find at all, the grave of Arthur.

The three graves at Cefn Celfi,
of which the muse told me –
the grave of Cynon, frowning roughly,
the graves of Cynfal and Cynfeli.

Gwell's grave is at Rhiw Felen.
Sawyl's grave, at Llangollen.
Llam y Bwlch's watched by Llorien.

The grave of Gwaeanwyn, of renown,
between the Llyfni and Llifon,
who yielded right to no-one.

Tryfan, Snowdonia:
'Bedwyr's grave is on Tryfan'

Henaint

Y ddeilen hon, neus cynired – gwynt
Gwae hi o'i thynged!
Hi hen, eleni ganed.

Old age
Anonymous, 9th century

This leaf, by the wind blown – along,
Woe to it fate's turn!
Now old, and but this year born.

Autumn, Snowdonia

The Age of Princes

It could all have been deleted. By the eleventh century, the Welsh-speaking kingdoms of the 'Old North' had ceased to exist, ground to dust by Scots and Angles and Norsemen, and the Welsh poetic tradition, like that of the Picts, could have been utterly lost, or at least truncated: but it wasn't.

Rather, the tradition demonstrated its remarkable facility for jumping from a sinking ship to one still afloat, and going somewhere. By the seventh century, it's apparent that the traditions of the Old North had been passed to present-day Wales, where they invigorated the local poetic heritage. In north-eastern Wales the Kingdom of Powys became the epicentre of a new cycle of poems about the struggle to beat off the burgeoning power of Mercia, and the heavy price paid, in death and suffering, for independence.

The locations had changed and the cast was different, but the ethos remained the same. It was still an heroic society, ruled by princes, maintained by force of arms and funded by largesse. The poems deliberately echo those of the Old North, because these princes were immensely proud, and wished to be identified with that older tradition of heroes and warriors. To secure a prominent place in that tradition by virtue of their deeds was essential to their prestige and confidence, even when the poetry grew archaic and almost incomprehensible: for it had served them and their fathers very well, and they saw no point in changing it. In that respect, they were very conservative.

New notes were being heard, however. There was an increasing interest in the individual's psychology, his or her personal feelings and response to events. There's also an interest in the environment: in the fleeting beauty of nature, the thoughts evoked by a seagull's flight, a withered leaf, or a shining, foam-flecked wave. Romantic love got to weave its enchantments and disappointments in verse, too. Also striding confidently to the poets' attention came another band of warriors, spiritual ones, in the persons of saints and priests, calling all to virtue and repentance, and putting to flight the armies of evil by prayer and miracles.

Castell Carreg Cennen – a Welsh stronghold

These were no pale curates, but men of royal blood and action, as ready to stand and lead as their sword-wielding brothers and cousins.

God is, of course, the ultimate patron, and in this period and subsequently never lacked the attentions of poets who would praise and supplicate Him, directly or through the Church's powerful and wealthy hierarchy of bishops and abbots. Neither would any good poet lack secular patrons: for Wales was divided and subdivided into a restless mosaic of kingdoms and domains, each with its ruler and royal family and court. To be of account, a prince would have to maintain a warband and a staff of officials including his chancellor, his doctor, his magistrate and, of course, at least one *pencerdd* or chief poet.

Such men of importance would have been entitled to sit in chairs, rather than on a stool or bench: and although that order has long passed away, the ultimate accolade for a Welsh poet is still to be awarded a chair. This period also sees the holding of the first *eisteddfodau*, meetings at which poets and musicians would assemble in order to compete for prizes, the most desirable being a post at court. The concept may have originated in Burgundy, but for all their conservatism, Welsh rulers weren't blind to new ideas which promoted their interests. Some poets, for their part, seem to have had an eye for better opportunities, switching patrons when necessity demanded or opportunity arose. Others remained faithful to their employers at all costs, sharing their tribulations and exile. In addition to Powys, the greatest centres of power were the kingdoms of Dyfed in the south-west and, increasingly, Gwynedd in the north-west.

Poems could be long or short, and delivered in a variety of forms ranging from the compact three-line, twenty-one syllable *englyn milwr* to long odes of nine and ten-syllable lines, all to the same rhyme. Apart from showering praise on their shield-shattering, Saxon-slaying patrons, poets would also thank them for gifts, mourn them and their wives and warriors, sing to their patron saints and recount their own amorous success and failures, to general amusement, no doubt. Princes could themselves take up the art, and in such works, free of the need to bolster someone else's image, we may have a clearer glimpse of what made a medieval ruler tick.

It has been argued, of course, that the poets were nothing but a claque of sycophants and spin doctors who portrayed a wildly idealized image of their employers, far removed from the cruelty, duplicity and military failure characteristic of so many of them. Perhaps the poets' comments on those matters weren't for the written record: but in any case, their job was to hold up before all a portrait of what a good ruler should be. If the hearers could then perceive a difference between what was portrayed and what was reality, then they could draw their own conclusions as to the fitness of the prince.

By the middle of the thirteenth century, Anglo-Norman incursions under the English crown, and the growing power of the Kings of Gwynedd, had virtually divided Wales into two spheres of influence. A final showdown was inevitable, and it came in 1282 with the killing of Llywelyn ap Gruffudd of Gwynedd by forces loyal to Edward I of England. This was a cataclysmic end to the old order, and the poets responded appropriately, lamenting the death of Llywelyn and his warband, even though there was now no prince to reward them for their songs. Opposition limped on for another few months, but after that, there's silence. How was the poetic tradition to survive this?

Rhuddlan: 'the red court'

Buddugoliaeth ieuenctid Gwynedd

Pan fai lawen frain, pan ddyfrysiai – waed,
      Pan wyar waryai,
    Pan rhyfel, pan rhuddid ei thai,
    Pan Rhuddlan, pan rhuddlys losgai,
Pan rhuddai rhuddfflam, fflemychai – hyd nef
      Yn addef ni noddai,
    Hawdd gweled goleulosg arnai
    O gaer wen geir ymyl Menai.
Trengisiant trydydd o Fai – trychanllong
      Yn y llynges fordai,
    A decant cynran a'i ciliai,
    Cynfarf heb un farf ar Fenai.

The victory of the youths of Gwynedd
Hywel ab Owain Gwynedd, fl. c. 1139 – 1167

When on the battlefield crows were happy,
When in such play, blood flowed quickly,
When there was war, its houses reddened by fire,
When Rhuddlan, the red court, was made a pyre,
When flames shot to heaven, and burned even redder,
At the settlement which could now give no shelter,
It was easy to see the bonfire's brightness
From the shores of Menai, from the fair fortress.
On the third day of May, came three hundred
Ships tall as buildings, a fleet which foundered:
At Menai they were sent off, defeated
By a thousand warriors, armed and unbearded.

I forwyn

Gwelais ar vorwyn uwyn vawrrydic,
Golwc diserchawc, syberw, keynmic,
Lliw goleu tonneu, taenverw gwenic,
Llanw ebyr a'r llyr lle ny mawrdric;
Mynych ymanvon dygyn gofyon dic
Y rof a riein, gannwyll ryuic,
Mel yd wyf yn kelu kallon yssic:
Ny mad gyrchawd gwenn gwely Eidic!

To a maiden
Cynddelw Brydydd Mawr, c. 1155 – c. 1195

I saw on a maiden, splendid, lovely,
A look of distain, proud and haughty.
Oh, shining wave! White foam of the sea,
Scattered and vanishing! Such was she.
Such painful and bitter thoughts did we
Exchange – how arrogant she could be! –
That I hide a bruised heart none may see:
And now she's in Eiddig's bed! Woe me!

Marwnad Llywelyn ap Gruffudd (*rhan*)

Pony welwch chwi hynt y gwynt ar glaw?
Pony welwch chwi r drei yn ymdaraw?
Pony welwch chwi r mor yn merwinaw yr tir?
Pony welwch chwi r gwir yn ymgyweiaw?
Pony welwch chwi r heul yn hwylaw r awyr?
Pony welwch chwi r syr wedyr syrthiaw?
Pony chredwch chwi y Duw, dynyadon ynvyt?
Pony welwch chwi r byt wdyr dydyaw?
Och yt attat ti Duw na daw mor tros dir!
Pas beth yn gedir y ohiriaw?

Nyt oes le y kyrcher rac carchar braw,
Nyt oes le y trigyer: och or trigyaw!
Nyt oes na chyngor, na chlo nac egor
Unfford y escor brwyn gyngor braw.

Pob teulu teilwng oed idaw,
pob kedwyr kedwynt adanaw.
Pob dengyn a dyngynt oe law,
pob gwledic, pob gwalt oed eidaw.
Pob cantref, pob tref ynt yn treidyaw,
pob tylwyth, pob llwyth yssyn llithraw.
Pob gwann, pob kadarn kadwet oe law,
pob mab yn y grut yssyn udaw.

Bychan lles oed ym am vyn twyllaw,
gadel penn arnaf heb penn araw.
Penn pan las ny bu gas gymraw;
penn pas las oedd lessach peidyaw;
penn milwr, penn molyant rac llaw,
penn dragon, penn dreic oed arnaw;

penn Llywelyn dec dygyn a vraw byt
bot pawl heaarn trwydaw;
penn varglwyd, poen dygyngwyd am daw,
pan veneit heb vanac aranw;
penn a vu berchen a barch naw canwlat
a naw canwled idaw;
penn teyrn, heyrn heeit oe law,
penn teyrn, walch balch bwlch y geifnaw;
penn teyrneid vleid vlaengar ganthaw,
penn teyrnef, nef y nawd arnaw!

The elegy of Llywelyn ap Gruffudd (*extract*)
Gruffudd ab yr Ynad Coch, c. 1282 – 83

Don't you see the wind and rain driving?
Don't you see the oak trees clashing?
Don't you see the sea clawing – at the land?
Don't you see the truth cowering?
Don't you see the sun sailing – through the sky?
Don't you see the stars falling?
Don't you believe in God, – foolish men?
Don't you see the world's imperiling?
Oh God, let the sea come covering – the land!
Why are we left remaining?

A memorial ceremony at Cilmeri,
where Llywelyn was killed

From the bonds of horror, there's no fleeing,
No place to linger, woe the lingering!
There's neither counsel, nor lock, nor opening,
No way to be rid of grim terror's reasoning.

Every worthy retinue was his following,
Every warrior under him remaining,
Every brave man by his hand swearing,
Every province, every homestead piercing,
Every family, every tribe is slipping,
Every babe in his cradle howling.

Little did I gain for my deceiving,
That I kept my head, and his head missing,
A head which no enemy feared its cutting,
A head which to cut was unbenefiting,
A warrior's head, worthy of praising,
He a hero's head, a dragon's head having,
Fair Llywelyn's head: oh, frightful thing – to the world,
On an iron pole, its transfixing,
My lord's head, woe my painful falling,
My soul's head, now unspeaking,
A lord nine hundred lands' homage owning – and he
Nine hundred feasts giving,
A king's head, his hand iron-sowing,

A proud royal falcon's head, breaches opening,
A royal wolf's head, forward thrusting:
May the Great Chief of Heaven be his safeguarding.

The Age of Noblemen

It survived by jumping ship, again. Though independence had been lost, Edward and his successors didn't delete the entire ruling caste, so long as they obeyed the law and paid taxes. There were no more princes, but there remained plenty of great nobles, wealthy churchmen and middling squires who had all of a prince's pride, and enough wealth to pay a poet to praise their lineage, broadcast their virtues and flatter their ambitions. The poets went calling.

Following the conquest, it seems to have taken a few decades for a new order to be established; but given time and stability, the tradition proved itself able to flower anew with astounding vigour. The poet Dafydd ap Gwilym burts onto the scene in the first half of the fourteenth century with a new kind of poetry: intimate, personal, self-mocking at times, and deeply influenced by a love of nature and women, which owes much to the Provençal tradition of troubadours and courtly love. He was as adept at turning out an ode in the old fashion as any, but his forte was the *cywydd*, a much more supple and lively poem of rhymed seven-syllable couplets, but just as capable of carrying a prolonged theme. Another increasingly popular form was the thirty-syllable, four line *englyn unodl union*, well suited to pithy, laconic observation, much like a Japanese *haiku*. There were over twenty other forms of varying length and complexity: but these two became, and remain, the mainstays of subsequent strict-metre poetic art.

Dafydd ap Gwilym was a brilliant innovator, recognized by his contemporaries and successors as one of the best Welsh poets ever. He quickly found followers who took this new style forward and outwards to cover all the fields and events where a poet's services were required, and beyond that into more personal expression and reflection. Alongside poems on long-familiar themes such as a high-class wedding, thanking a patron for a gift, stirring a nobleman to arms or asking the intercession of a saint, we now have laments on the death of a child, bawdy comedy and satirical contests with other poets. Some poets were themselves landed gentry, others wholly dependent on patrons. Unless permanently engaged, poets would go abroad at set seasons (usually coincident with major holidays such as Christmas), travelling from one household to another in hope of employment, bringing news and gossip, offering compositions and picking up commissions for completion by the next visit.

These poets were very aware of their high status, and guarded their craft and reputations jealously. Novices would seek to learn from regarded masters, who trained the cream of the emerging talent. The remainder were dismissed as *clêr* ('flies'), mere rhymesters who'd compose for anyone – even commoners – and for paltry reward. It's a moot point as to whether the poets would actually recite their own compositions: that may have been the function of a *datgeiniad*, a reciter, accompanied by a harpist. Patrons would employ poets in ritual exchanges of gifts with one another, and kept albums of poems sung in their family's honour, or simply those which appealed to them. This desire for a permanent record meant that more and more poems were set down, often with their authors' names, so that we now have a corpus of thousands of such works, by hundreds of poets. Most remain unpublished.

There is a way in which poetry is well suited to the Welsh, for we've never had much in the way of money. With money one can build palaces, stage operas, fashion jewellery and generally express oneself artistically at conspicuous expense. Poetry, storytelling and music, however, can produce entertainment out of very limited funds, and in a culture which so appreciates eloquence and wit, and is so concerned to remember and preserve, the poet's art is the very highest. Once heard, every single composition, famous or unregarded, deathless or ephemeral, becomes a contribution to an ever-growing body of work, an edifice as huge and glorious, in its way, as any cathedral. The foundations are buried, but solid; the basic plan and lower courses are Romanesque, the work of a people who knew beauty, but gave priority to strength; and during the high Middle Ages were added soaring Gothic work, light and brilliantly coloured by similies and cadences as by stained glass. This is Wales' Chartres, its Lincoln, its Cologne: but unlike them, it's a continuing work.

Not, however, without alterations, for changes are always afoot. In the fifteenth century the social structure of Wales was severely disturbed by the revolt of Owain Glyndŵr and the Wars of the Roses, but still the poets flourished. More disruptive by far was the advent of centralized rule from London following 1485, with increasing pressure, deliberate and incidental, on the gentry to attend court, act as agents of the Crown, and become Anglicized. Becoming estranged from their own people and culture, they ceased to provide patronage. A few maintained the old ways, but otherwise the poets found themselves out of demand. This is reflected not only in a decline in the number of professional poets, but also in the quality of the verse, which becomes more hackneyed and less accomplished as the sixteenth century draws to a close. The ship was sinking again.

A Welsh noble court, late medieval (Tretŵr)

Moliant Ieuan ap Gruffudd Foel (*rhan*)

Cyfaill grym y sy'm nis amheuir,
Cyfaill beirddion yw fy llyw llafnhir,
Cyfaill hynod glod a gludir – fwyfwy,
Cyfaill arlwy rwy ni rygeblir.

In praise of Ieuan ap Gruffudd Foel (*extract*)
Llywelyn Brydydd Hoddnant, fl. c. 1280 – 1330

I've a strong friend who's not doubted,
Long-bladed prince, poets' comrade,
A friend of fame broadcasted – all the more,
Friend not scorned, who's open-handed.

Morfudd

Ni pheidiaf â Morfudd, hoff adain – serchog
Pes archai Bab Rhufain;
Hoyw-wawl ddeurudd haul ddwyrain,
Oni ddêl y mêl o'r main.

Morfudd
Dafydd ap Gwilym, fl. c. 1340 – 1350

Though the Pope of Rome should thunder
My true love I'll not surrender,
Morfudd fair, my dawn-hued beauty
'Till the very rocks gush honey.

Mis Mai a mis Tachwedd

Hawddamor, glwysgor glasgoed,
Fis Mai haf, canys mau hoed,
Cadarn farchog, serchog sâl,
Cadwynwyrdd feistr coed anial,
Cyfaill cariad ac adar,
Cof y serchogion a'u câr,
Cennad nawugain cynnadl,
Caredig urddedig ddadl.
Mawr a fudd, myn Mair, ei fod,
Mai, fis difai, yn dyfod
Ar fryd arddelw, frwd urddas,
Yn goresgyn pob glyn glas.
Gwasgod praff, gwisgad priffyrdd,
Gwisgai bob lle â'i we wyrdd.
Pan ddêl yn ôl rhyfel rhew,
Pill doldir, pall adeildew –
Digrif fydd, mau grefydd grill,
Llwybr obry lle bu'r Ebrill –
Y daw ar uchaf blaen dâr
Caniadau cywion adar,
A chog ar fan pob rhandir,
A chethlydd a hoywddydd hir,
A nïwl gwyn yn ael gwynt
Yn diffryd canol dyffrynt,

May and November

Green chancel of the woods, fair May,
How I've longed to see this day!
Green-chained master of the trees,
Mighty knight, and lover's ease,
Friend to love and birds art thou,
And lovers' memory, I trow,
Messanger of trysts past counting,
Dignified and loving meeting.
By the Virgin, it's good cheer
That perfect May should now be here
To claim and conquer green glens all
With warm dignity withall.
His thick mantle clothes the ways,
His greenstuff dresses every place.
When he comes from icy contest
(meadow's fortress, woven closest)
Then like birdsong, I'll send praise
Heavenwards along the ways
Which April trod; on oaken branches
Little birds will lift their voices.
The cuckoo's call on high is heard,
There's long fine days for singing bird;
Before the wind, the white mists stand
A-guarding of the valley land.

Ac wybren loyw hoyw brynhawn,
A glaswydd aml a glwyswawn,
Ac adar aml ar goedydd,
Ac irddail ar wiail wŷdd,
A chof fydd Forfudd f'eurferch,
A chyffro saith nawtro serch.

Annhebig i'r mis dig du
A gerydd i bawb garu,
A bair tristlaw a byrddydd
A gwynt i ysbeilio gwŷdd,
A llesgedd, breuoledd braw,
A llaesglog a chenllysglaw,
Ac annog llanw ac annwyd,
Ac mewn naint llifeiriaint llwyd,
A dwyn sôn mewn afonydd,
A llidio a duo dydd,
Ac awyr drymled ledoer
A'i lliw yn gorchuddio'r lloer.
Dêl iddo, rhyw addo rhwydd,
Deuddrwg am ei wladeiddrwydd.

Fine afternoons, gossamer fair,
Blue skies, and green trees everywhere;
So many birds among the trees,
Every bough now sporting leaves
As thoughts of my bright Morfudd move
My mind to all the thrills of love.

How unlike mean, black November
Which frowns dark on every lover,
With rain so sad and days so short,
And gales which rob the trees to nought,
And sluggishness, and weakness pale,
Long cloaks, and storms of sleet and hail,
Bringing icy cold and flooding,
And brown rivers overflowing;
Many rivulets so noisy,
And the daytime dark and angry,
Heavy skies whose freezing blast
Leaves the moon so overcast.
Easy to say: but twice may he
Suffer for discourtesy.

Moel Hebog – wintry sunset
'black November/which frowns dark on every lover'

Henaint (*rhan*)

Esgeiriau yn ysgyrion
Y sydd, fal dwy ffawydd ffon.
Ysgwyddau anosgeiddig
A chorff heb na lliw na chig.
Rhyfedd yw f'ais i'w rhifo,
Fal clwyd lle tynnwyd y to.
Gleiniau fy nghefn a drefnwyd
Yn gerrig craig neu'n gyrc rhwyd.
Mal ffustiau, gïau gwywon,
Yw'r ddau fraich ar y ddwy fron,
A'm dwylaw, fu'n adeiliog,
Mal delwau cigweiniau cog.
Mae'n brudd y grudd ac yn grych
Mal y gwydr amlwg edrych,
A'm llygad ym mhell eigiawn
'Y mhen, ni ad im hun iawn.
Gŵr oerach nag Eryri
A Berwyn wyf, i'm barn i;
Ni thyn na chlydwr na thân
Na dillad f'annwyd allan.
Crynedig i'm croen ydwyf,
Crynfa deilen aethnen wyf.

Old age (*extract*)
Ieuan Brydydd Hir, *c. 1450*

My two shattered shins, they each
Are like a spindly stick of beech,
My shoulders slope, and I'm so lean
And pallid, I can scarce be seen!
My ribs are countable, each one,
Like rafters where the roof has gone,
My vertebrae like stones are set,
Or like cork floats along a net.
My arms (oh, how my tendons wither!)
Are like two threshing flails together,
And my two hands, once mighty, look
Like a scullion's clawed flesh-hook.
My cheeks are grey and furrowed – see,
The mirror shows it obviously!
My eyes are sunk into my head,
I'm robbed of sleep when I'm abed;
I think I'm colder in my chills
Than Berwyn or Snowdonia's hills.
No cosiness, no fire, no clothing
Can rid me of this cold: I'm freezing!
In my very skin I quake,
And like an aspen leaf, I shake.

Diolch am ŵn coch (*rhan*)

... Y gŵn a gad gan y gŵr,
Fal gŵn o fâl y gwinwr.
Ydd wyf yn debyg i'w ddwyn
I danllwyth mewn rhydynllwyn.
Llawenydd, nid llai unnos,
Lle cad rhodd lliw cawad rhos,
Lliw ceirioes haf, lliw cwyr sêl,
Lliw gwaed carw llygaid cwrel.

Lle delo bun i unoed
Llwynog wyf mewn llwyn o goed.
Os llechu'n fwyn yn nhrwyn rhiw,
Ogfaenllwyn a gaf unlliw.
Da iawn y'm heurwyd o ŵn
A bynar ar ei bennwn.
Bryn rhudd, mab barwn a'i rhoes,
Bron ragrith, brynar egroes.
Golud iso gwlad Esyllt
Goddail, a gwisg Gwyddel gwyllt.
Gweddus im, mal y gwyddoch,
Gael dwyn y criawol-lwyn coch.
Tebyg wyf, herwydd tŷb gŵr,
I'r pentis wrth dŷ'r peintiwr.

Thanks for a red gown (*extract*)
Ieuan Du'r Bilwg, *c.* 1470

... The man with this gown did me dress,
A gown of grapes from vintner's press.
When I wear it, I'll be taken
For a bonfire in the bracken.
Shower of roses – oh, delight! –
A gift for more than just one night.
Summer cherries, wax for sealing,
Coral spots, stag's blood resembling.

When a maiden waits for me
In a brake, a fox I'll be.
On the leeside, at my ease,
I'm as one with hawthorn trees.
Well I'm gilded by this gown,
A banner on its pennant sown;
Red hill, gift of baron's own,
False hill, tilth with rose-hips sown,
Wealth of Esyllt's Land, no less,
Young leaves, and wild Irish dress.
As you know, with dignity
I wear this red rowan tree.
All compare me, as I go,
To a painter's studio.

Y mae marched y gwledydd
Yn y gwlân hwn i'm galw'n hydd;
Yn hwrdd y'm galwant yn hir
Croen euraid, ni'm cryn oerir.
Arfer a wnaf o glera
Y fforest aur â ffris da,
Ac arnaf, fal iarll Gwernan,
Y saif mil o syfi mân.
Gweled a wneir o'r gilarth
Grawn yr yw ar groen yr arth.
Un llun yw'r gŵn, pennwn parch,
Ac un lliw â gŵn Llywarch.
Edling â mi a odlir
Gleddau tân, arglwydd y tir.
Rhyfedd yw yr haf heddiw
Gan bob un fy llun a'm lliw.

Mi af i dafarn y medd
I'r lle uchaf o'r llechwedd,
I'm lliw aruthr, i'm llwyrwisg,
I ferched weled y wisg.

In this wool, the women all
Far and near, a stag me call;
They call me a ram in fleece
Of gold. Now I'll never freeze!
All in a forest's golden glow
In good frieze, I'll singing go,
And on me, as on Gwernan's laird,
A thousand strawberries stand bared.
I'll be seen from yon hill-side
Yew-fruit on a brown bear's hide,
So like (pennon of renown)
The colour of old Llywarch's gown.
The heir of this homeland's lord
Clad me in a fiery sword.
All the folk, this day of summer,
Wonder at my form and colour.

I'll go high, and higher still,
To the mead-house on the hill.
In my glorious attire
So that women can admire.

Hoen gwawr haf o'i hystafell
A'm dengys â bys o bell,
Fal dangos draw, o daw dydd,
Llid nawawr, lleuad newydd,
A thaeru, ail waith aeron,
Mai'r ddraig goch er mawrddrwg hon.

Lliw da oedd yn llaw y dyn
A'i lliwiodd dros orllewyn;
Y lliwydd gwinau llawen
Lliwid Duw e'n ŵr llwyd hen.

One like a dawning summer's day
Will point me out from far away,
As one points out (oh, fiery noon!)
The ruddy rise of the new moon,
Swearing that a scarlet dragon
(so like berries) brings destruction!

Such good dye did dyer use
Who dyed the gown with sunset's hues:
May God dye that happy dyer
With old grey hairs, long to expire!

Marwnad Siôn y Glyn

Un mab oedd degan i mi;
Dwynwen! Gwae'i dad o'i eni!
Gwae a edid, o gudab,
I boeni mwy heb un mab!
Fy nwy ais, farw fy nisyn,
Y sy'n glaf am Siôn y Glyn.
Udo fyth yr ydwyf fi
Am benáig mabinogi.

Afal pêr ac aderyn
A garai'r gwas, a gro gwyn;
Bwa o flaen y ddraenen,
Cleddau digon brau o bren.
Ofni'r bib, ofni'r bwbach,
Ymbil â'i fam am bêl fach.
Canu i bawb acen o'i ben,
Canu 'ŵo' er cneuen.
Gwneuthur moethau, gwenieithio,
Sorri wrthyf fi wnâi fo,
A chymod er ysglodyn
Ac er dis a garai'r dyn.

Och nad Siôn, fab gwirion gwâr,
Sy'n ail oes i Sain Lasar!

The elegy for his only son, Siôn y Glyn
Lewis Glyn Cothi, fl. c. 1447 – 1486

One son was my only treasure,
oh, Saint Dwynwen, woe his father!
Woe his birth, that I remain
sonless! Love's displaced by pain.
My two flanks are smitten by
the death of Siôn y Glyn, my die;
now I'm one who ever wails
for a prince of boyhood tales.

The lad who loved a fragrant apple,
and a bird, and a white pebble,
a bow that was of quickthorn made,
and swords of fragile, wooden blade.
He feared the bagpipe, feared the spectre,
and for a ball he'd beg his mother.
To everyone he's singing go,
and for a nut, he'd sing 'oo-oh';
he'd practice love and flattery,
and just as soon, fall out with me;
then make it up, to be rewarded
with a chip or die he'd fancied.

Woe that Siôn, sweet, innocent son,
could not a Lazarus become!

Beuno a droes iddo saith
Nefolion yn fyw eilwaith;
Gwae eilwaith, fy ngwir galon,
Nad oes wyth rhwng enaid Siôn.

O Fair, gwae fi o'i orwedd!
A gwae fy ais gau ei fedd!
Yngo y saif angau Siôn
Yn ddeufrath yn y ddwyfron:
Fy mab, fy muarth baban,
Fy mron, fy nghalon, fy nghân,
Fy mryd cyn fy marw ydoedd,
Fy mardd doeth, fy mreuddwyd oedd;
Fy nhegan oedd, fy nghannwyll,
Fy enaid teg, fy un twyll,
Fy nghyw yn dysgu fy nghân,
Fy nghae Esyllt, fy nghusan,
Fy nerth, gwae fi yn ei ôl!
Fy ehedydd, fy hudol,
Fy serch, fy mwa, fy saeth,
F'ymbiliwr, fy mabolaeth.

Siôn sy'n danfon i'w dad
Awch o hiraeth a chariad.
Yn iach wên ar fy ngenau!
Yn iach chwerthin o'r min mau!

Saint Beuno brought no less than seven
back to life, who'd been to heaven;
woe my heart, again I moan,
that the eighth could not be Siôn!

Mary! Woe to me his lying!
Woe my flank at his grave's filling!
Siôn's death stands close, in all its pain,
twice stabbing in the breast again.
My little ember of diversion,
my breast, my heart, my song, my son.
My one desire before my passing,
my dream, my poet of great learning,
my very candle, and my bauble,
my fair soul, my one betrayal,
my chick, who learnt my poetry,
my precious brooch, my kiss was he,
my strength, woe me that he's gone!
My skylark, and my magic one,
my bow, my arrow, my caress,
my supplicant, my youthfulness.

Siôn sends to his father pain
in love and longing to remain.
On my lips, there's no more smiling,
in my mouth, there's no more laughing.

Yn iach mwy diddanwch mwyn!
Ac yn iach i gnau echwyn!
Ac yn iach bellach i'r bêl!
Ac yn iach ganu'n uchel!
Ac yn iach, fy nghâr arab
Iso'n fy myw, Siôn fy mab!

No more will he come a-begging
nuts; there's no more merrymaking.
Playing ball is over and done,
and singing out aloud is gone.
Whilst I below on earth do dwell,
my darling friend, my Siôn, farewell!

Gofyn march (*rhan*)

Trem hydd am gywydd a gais
trwynbant, yn troi'n ei unbais;
ffriw yn dal ffrwyn o daliwn,
ffroen y sy gau fal ffoen gwn;
ffroen arth a chyffro'n ei ên,
ffrwyn a ddeil ei ffriw'n ddolen.
Llygaid fal dwy ellygen
llymion byw'n llamu'n ei ben.
Dwyglust feinion afloynydd
dail saets wrth ei dâl y sydd.
Trwsio fal goleuo glain
y bu wydrwr ei bedrain.
Ei flew fal sidan newydd,
a'i rawn o liw gwawn y gwŷdd.
Sidan ym mhais ehedydd,
siamled yn hws am lwdn hydd.

Ail y carw, olwg gorwyllt,
a'i draed yn gwau drwy dân gwyllt.
Dylifo heb ddwylo'dd oedd,
neu wau sidan, nes ydoedd.

Requesting a horse (*extract*)
Tudur Aled, c. 1465 – 1525

...He seeks an ode about one who
has a stag's look, and dimpled, too,
about the nose, and who can spin
within the tunic of his skin.
A snout on which we put a bridle,
with hollow nostril, a gun's muzzle,
a bear's nostril, quivering chin,
with bridle looped to put it in.
His eyes are of a lively glance,
like two pears in his head, they dance;
his slim and twitching ears resemble
two sage-leaves set at either temple.
So polished is his hinder part,
like beadwork of a glazier's art.
A coat of newest silk he wears,
with gossamer of trees for hairs,
all silken like a skylark's blouse,
a young stag that in samite's housed.

Like a stag of aspect dire,
with feet that weave through flying fire,
without hands, he'd weave with skill,
or even braid silk, finer still.

Ystwyro cwrs y daran,
a thuthio pan fynno'n fân.
A bwrw naid i'r wybr a wnâi
ar hyder yr ehedai.
Cnyw praff yn cnöi priffordd,
cloch y ffair, ciliwch o'i ffordd!
Sêr neu fellt ar sarn a fydd
ar godiad yr egwydydd.
Drythyll ar bedair wyth-hoel,
gwreichionen o ben pob hoel.
Dirwynnwr fry draw'n y fron,
deil i'r haul dalau'r hoelion.
Gwreichion a gair ohonyn'
gwnïwyd wyth bwyth ymhob un.
Ei arial a ddyfalwn
i elain coch o flaen cŵn.
Yn ei fryd nofio'r ydoedd
nwyfol iawn anifail oedd.
O gyrrir draw i'r gweirwellt
ni thyr â'i garn wyth o'r gwellt.

Neidiwr dros afon ydoedd,
naid yr iwrch rhag y neidr oedd.
Wynebai a fynnai fo,
pe'r trawst, ef a'i praw trosto.

Like the thunder when he courses,
and trots finely, when he pleases;
he could leap into the sky,
and with confidence could fly.
Sturdy colt, that eats the highway,
first in the fair: out of his way!
From the roadway, stars and lightning
will fly at his fetlocks' rising.
Four eights' nails – he's spirited –
with a spark at each nail's head.
He up yonder at the run,
showing nailheads to the sun,
and from them the sparks are struck,
each one with eight stitches stuck.
We compare his lively bounds
to a red fawn fleeing hounds,
and at swim he'd like to be,
such a spirited beast is he!
If taken out to graze, not eight
grass-blades would break beneath his weight.

At the river, he's a leaper,
like a roebuck from a viper.
Any obstacle he'd face,
any bar, he'd clear at pace.

Nid rhaid, er peri neidio,
dur fyth wrth ei dor efô.
Dan farchog bywiog, di-bŵl,
ef a wyddiad ei feddwl.
Draw os gyrrir dros gaered,
gorwydd yr arglwydd a red.
Llamu draw lle mwya'r drain,
llawn ergyd yn Llan Eurgain.
Gorau 'rioed, gyrru i redeg,
march da am arwain merch deg.
Mae'n f'aros yma forwyn
merch deg, pe ceid march i'w dwyn.

To make him jump, there'd be no need
to prick steel into this steed.
With a lively, clever knight,
he would know his mind, alright.
Set to jump a wall out yonder,
the lord's horse will prove a runner.
Leaper where the thorns are thick,
in Northop he gives such a kick!
Best of all, when set to run,
to fetch a fair maid, he's the one.
A maiden now awaits me here,
had I a horse to bring my dear.

Darfu am nawdd

Rhodio plwy Beuno y bûm – heb ginio,
Heb gynnal yr oeddym;
O dai wythwr y deuthum,
P'le bynnag, bolwag y bûm.

An end to patronage

Edward Maelor, fl. 1567 – 1603

I wandered Beuno's parish – without food,
And was set to perish;
At eight doors, got not one dish
Anywhere: so I famish.

Folk verses

From the seventeenth century onwards, Wales had, effectively, no indigenous ruling class. Most of those in charge were either English or Anglicized, and had no interest in the aristocratic poetic tradition. It had but one remaining refuge: among the common folk.

Which isn't to say that they didn't already have their own traditions of poetry and song. We've caught a few glimpses of it already, accidentally or casually included in manuscripts of more exalted verse: but new social trends and technological developments over the next two hundred years meant that the songs and poems of farmers, labourers, craftsmen and housewives were now recorded and widely circulated for the first time.

The old caste of professional poets gradually died out, but some of the lesser gentry maintained an interest in their works. Whereas in England the advent of printing had resulted in an explosion of books, Wales had no presses: any Welsh book had to be printed in England, and subject to strict censorship. So in Wales, the Renaissance interest in the works of ancient authors manifested itself not in books, but in the copying and collection of old manuscripts. This 'safe' form of nationalism could be pursued without official disapproval, and led to the formation of significant libraries of poetry, available for further transmission and publication when circumstances allowed.

Although the poets now found themselves in reduced circumstances, they didn't lose their creativity. Handicraft or trade still gave them time and opportunity to compose, and they remained an integral part of a society which still required their services as celebrants and commentators. They learnt to better their living by adapting to the fashions of the age. A lengthy *cywydd* would have few takers, and the old repertoire of harp music had all but died out: but newer, freer forms of poetry and music were now in vogue (many originating in England or on the Continent), and these were readily adapted into Welsh. Their appeal was much enhanced by use of the old alliterative techniques, and a knowledge of the basics of the high poetic tradition remained *de rigeur* for any serious versifier.

Others, less ambitious, made do with short forms such as the *pennill* ('verse') of four lines of eight syllbles each, with an AABB or ABAB rhyme; and the *triban* of four lines of 7,7,8 and 7 syllables, with an AAB, B (internal) A rhyme. Their anonymous authors did not aspire to anything other than the expression of their own feelings and the amusement or education of other members of their kin and community, but it says much for their success that their works have been kept and transmitted (orally and in writing) in their hundreds.

A strong new impetus to poetry came from the Protestant Reformation. Odes to the Virgin and saints were out, but as Luther realized, song was good for raising and maintaining awareness of the need for personal salvation. Psalms were versified and tunes provided, and from this there gradually developed a tradition of hymnody which by the end of the eighteenth century had become a prime medium of poetic expression. We little appreciate today how interested our forefathers were in matters of belief, how much thought and time they devoted to it: but the great (and still growing) corpus of Welsh hymnody stands testament to their piety and devotion.

Many were concerned enough to teach others to read specifically in order to give them direct access to Scripture and other godly writings, with the result that by the end of the eighteenth century Wales was possibly the most literate country in Europe. The Welsh were a sizeable audience, needing to be fed, and with the slackening of press restrictions, increasing numbers of pamphlets and volumes of hymns and other poetry provided for a growing demand.

Not that it was all religious. Ballads were much in vogue, providing news, comment, and entertainment cheaply and memorably. There also arose a tradition of popular drama, the *anterliwt* ('interlude'), substantial productions in metre and rhyme giving folk a chance to laugh and cry at the deeds of stock characters, with topical references and satire thrown in. As with the ballads, some of these 'interludes' could be rather *risqué*, but the rising influence of Nonconformity led to a general toning down of this ancient aspect of the poet's repertoire. Not its extinction, though. Simlarly frowned upon by the respectable were the *eisteddfodau*, no longer held in mansions, but rather in a convenient pub at a date previously advertised in the latest almanac or ballad-sheet. Here the old tradition of poetic contest in verse and song hobbled on, aided by liberal amounts of ale. Open to all comers, they gave a competitive impetus to composition and transmission at a time when other support was lacking.

When that support did reappear, it was from a rather unexpected quarter. Wales had no large cities, no centres of population where enough wealth could be concentrated to permit appreciable patronage of the arts. England, and specifically London, did: and it was to there that many Welshmen and women gravitated to further their careers as members of the nascent middle class of officials and tradesmen. Among these were people who had a deep interest in antiquities and the poetic tradition, and were now inclined to use their resources to preserve what remained and promote what was lacking. Members of expatriate societies like the *Cymmrodorion* and *Gwyneddigion* patronized those they perceived to be best talented; organized *eisteddfodau* and competitons, and promoted publication. Their tastes determined what kind of poetry would be considered worthiest for a long time afterwards: an elevated, consciously old-fashioned imitation of the medieval style, purged of rudeness, Roman Catholicism and tactless sentiments concerning the English.

The early seventeenth century had brought crisis, which the tradition had survived by finding refuge among commoners and *dilettanti*. At the close of the eighteenth century it was set to flourish anew in an era of unprecedented change, for it was proving to be very adaptable.

Hen benillion

1.
Mi af i'r eglwys ddydd Sul nesaf,
A than raff y gloch mi eisteddaf;
Ac mi edrycha' â chil fy llygad
Pwy sy'n edrych ar fy nghariad.

2.
O f'anwylyd, cyfod frwynen,
Ac ymafael yn ei deupen;
Yn ei hanner tor hi'n union,
Fel y torraist ti fy nghalon.

3.
On'd ydyw hi'n rhyfeddod,
Fod dannedd merch yn darfod,
Ond tra bo ynddi anadl chwyth
Ni dderfydd byth mo'i thafod?

4.
Blin yw caru yma ac acw,
Blin bod heb y blinder hwnnw;
Ond o'r blinderau, blinaf blinder,
Cur annifyr, caru'n ofer.

Folk verses
Anonymous, 18th – 19th century

1.
When I'm next in church, I hope
To sit back by the belfry rope,
And see, by surreptitious peeping,
Who should gaze upon my darling.

2.
Take a bulrush by both ends,
Force it, dearest, 'till it bends.
Then see how it snaps apart:
That's just how you broke my heart.

3.
Isn't it amazing?
A woman's teeth wear out,
But while she lives and breathes, her tongue
Remains forever stout.

4.
For all courting's toil and trouble,
Better that, than to be single.
Yet they loudest do complain
Who go courting, all in vain.

5.

Tebyg ydyw'r delyn dyner
I ferch wen a'i chnawd melysber;
Wrth ei theimlo mewn cyfrinach,
Fe ddaw honno'n fwynach, fwynach.

6.

Afon Conwy'n llifo'n felyn,
Mynd â choed y maes i'w chanlyn;
Ar ei gwaelod mi rof drithro
Cyn y trof fy nghariad heibio.

7.

Pa waeth imi lodes wledig
Gyda'r nos na merch fonheddig?
Fe eill honno fod yn fwynach,
Ond bod crys y llall yn feinach.

8.

Mae'r merched bach eleni
Yn cneua'r hyd y perthi;
Fe ddala i cyn diwedd Mai,
Bydd lla'th gan rai o'r rheini.

5.

A girl, the finest of all things,
Is just like a harp and strings.
Set to practice in your chamber:
Soon the music's all the sweeter.

6.

See the Conwy in full flow,
See the trees and branches go.
On its bed three turns I'll make
Rather than my love forsake.

7.

You can keep your high-born lady:
I prefer a rustic lassie.
Not as gentle, but come sunset
Unencumbered by a corset.

8.

All the little girls are flocking
To the woods and groves a-nutting.
I bet some of them, come May,
Will be in the family way.

Llanrwst: 'See the Conwy in full flow'

9.
Dau lanc ifanc aeth i garu,
Gyda'r afon ar i fyny;
Un â'i wn, a'r llall â'i gledde',
Cysgod bedwen trodd nhw adre.

10.
Hir yw'r ffordd a maith yw'r mynydd
O Gwm Mawddwy i Drawsfynydd;
Ond lle bo 'wyllys mab i fyned,
Fe wêl y rhiw yn oriwaered.

11.
Trwm yw'r plwm, a thrwm yw'r cerrig,
Trom yw calon pob dyn unig;
Trymaf peth tan haul a lleuad
Canu'n iach lle byddo cariad.

12.
Tri pheth sy'n anodd imi,
Cyfri'r sêr pan fo hi'n rhewi,
Rhoi fy llaw ar gwr y lleuad,
A gwybod meddwl f'annwyl gariad.

9.
Two brave lads set out a-courting
With the river's waters rising.
One with gun, the other, cutlass:
Birch tree's shadow scared them witless.

10.
It's a long and lonely slog
Over hill and moor and bog,
But where passion gives the lead,
A young man's feet soon pick up speed.

11.
Heavy is lead, and heavy is stone,
Heavy the heart of he who's alone,
Heaviest of all things under the sky,
To be in love, and say goodbye.

12.
Three things beyond my doing,
To touch the moon by stretching,
To count the frosty stars aglow,
And know your mind, my darling.

13.
Croeso'r gwanwyn tawel cynnar,
Croeso'r gog a'i llawen lafar;
Croeso'r tes i rodio'r gweunydd,
A gair llon, ac awr llawenydd.

14.
Pan fo seren yn rhagori,
Fe fydd pawb â'i olwg arni;
Pan ddêl unwaith gwmwl drosti,
Ni fydd mwy o sôn amdani.

15.
Pe buasai'r brag a'r berman
A'r hops heb ddod i'r unman,
A ffiol fach a'r bib a'r pot,
Mi fuasai 'nghot i'n gyfan.

16.
Yng ngwaelod Cwm y Rhondda
Mae pwll sy'n un o'r dyfna
Lle clywir gaffers, dyna'r gwir,
Yn rheci gwŷr Ostrelia.

13.
Welcome, tender early Spring,
Welcome all the birds that sing,
Welcome, sunshine on our ways,
Loving words, and happy days.

14.
Brilliant star up there on high,
You catch everybody's eye.
Once a cloud obscures your kind,
You'll be out of sight and mind.

15.
If it weren't for malt and water,
Brewer's yeast and hops so bitter,
Black tobacco, pipe and matches,
I'd not be in rags and patches.

16.
Never was a Rhondda shaft
Sunk so deep by miners' craft.
On each shift, upon my soul,
We fight Australians for the coal.

Bugeilio'r gwenith gwyn

Mi sydd fachgen ifanc ffôl
Yn byw yn ôl ei ffansi,
Myfi'n bugeilio'r gwenith gwyn,
Ac arall yn ei fedi.
Pam na ddeui ar fy ôl
Ryw ddydd ar ôl ei gilydd?
Gwaith 'rwy'n dy weld, y feinir fach,
Yn lanach, lanach beunydd.

Glanach, glanach wyt bob dydd,
Neu fi â'm ffydd sydd ffolach;
Er mwyn y Gŵr a wnaeth dy wedd,
Dod im drugaredd bellach.
Cwn yma'th ben, gwêl acw draw,
Rho imi'th law wen dirion;
Gwaith yn dy fynwes bert ei thro
Mae allwedd clo fy nghalon.

Tra fo dŵr y môr yn hallt,
A thra fo 'ngwallt yn tyfu,
A thra fo calon dan fy mron,
Mi fydda'n ffyddlon iti;
Dywed imi'r gwir heb gêl,
A rho dan sêl d'atebion,
P'un ai myfi ai arall, Gwen,
Sydd orau gen dy galon?

Tending the golden wheat
Wil Hopcyn, 18th century

I'm a young and foolish lad,
Who lives just as he fancies,
A-tending of the golden wheat
Whilst others reap its bounties.
Won't you come and follow me
Today, or some day after?
Because I see thee, lovely lass,
Becoming daily fairer.

Aye, fairer, fairer by the day
Unless I'm sore mistaken:
Oh, for His sake, who made thy face,
Give me some little token.
Raise thy head, behold and see,
Let our hands be united,
For in thy bosom's rise and fall
My heart's key lies enfolded.

As long as brine fills up the deep,
As long as hair grows on me,
As long as my heart pulses on,
I shall be faithful to thee.
Tell me now, the truth, whole truth,
And sign and seal your answer,
Is it me, or someone else,
Who makes thy heart beat faster?

Henffych well

Henffych well, fy hen gyfeillion,
O Fôn ac Arfon ac ym Meirion,
Lle mae sẁn a suo tannau,
Yn eich mwynder cofiwch finnau.

Yn eich cwmni mi fûm lawen,
Yn eich plith mi fûm ben-hoeden.
Ni feddyliais o feddalwch
Y dôi diwedd ar ddifyrrwch.

Dyddiau f'ieuenctid a'm bwytasant,
Rhwng fy mysedd diangasant;
Gwedi bwrw 'mlodau gwynion
Dacw'r ffrwyth yn blant ac wyrion.

Fe ddaw'r rhain 'run modd â minnau,
Rhai'n dwyn dail a rhai'n dwyn blodau,
Rhai'n dwyn ffrwyth hyd ddiwedd amser, –
Ni wnaeth Duw un peth yn ofer.

Farewell now
Anonymous, ?18th century

Farewell now, my old companions,
Of the western hills and islands,
Where the sweet harp whispers softly,
May your dearest thoughts be of me.

When among you, I was happy,
I was queen of dance and party,
In my folly, little knowing,
That the good times had an ending.

Gone, my youth and all its pleasures,
Gone, like water through my fingers,
And my petals having fallen,
There's the fruit, my children's children.

Some in leaf, and some in flower,
Some in fruit for ever after.
Whether leaf or fruit or blossom,
All's according to God's wisdom.

Ymlid angau

Ar ryw noswaith yn fy ngwely,
Ar hyd y nos yn ffaelu cysgu,
Gan fod fy meddwl yn ddiama'
Yn cydfeddwl am fy siwrna'.

Galw am gawg a dŵr i 'molchi,
Gan ddisgwyl hynny i'm sirioli,
Ond cyn rhoi deigryn ar fy ngruddiau
Ar fin y cawg mi welwn Angau.

Mynd i'r eglwys i weddïo,
Gan dybio'n siŵr na ddeuai yno;
Ond cyn im godi oddi ar fy ngliniau
Ar ben y fainc mi welwn Angau.

Mynd i siambar glós i ymguddio,
Gan dybio'n siŵr na ddeuai yno,
Ond er cyn closied oedd y siambar
Angau ddaeth o dan y ddaear.

Mynd i'r môr a dechrau rhwyfo,
Gan dybio'n siŵr na fedrai nofio,
Ond cyn im fyn'd dros llyfnion donnau
Angau oedd y capten llongau.

Death's pursuit
Anonymous, ?18th century

One night as I lay a-bed,
Thoughts were tumbling in my head,
No sleep quelled their disarray,
As I dwelt upon my way.

I took water in a bowl,
Thinking to refresh my soul:
Ere I'd wet a finger tip,
Death stood at the basin's lip.

I went to the church to pray,
Thinking that he'd keep away:
Hardly had I bent a knee,
Death was sitting next to me.

I took refuge in a room,
Thinking to escape my doom:
Though the locks and bolts were sound,
Death rose up from underground.

I took oars and set to skim,
Thinking that he couldn't swim:
Hardly had I left dry land,
Captain Death was in command.

Death on the church rood screen, Llaneilian

Ffarwel, ferched, ffarwel, feibion,
Ffarwel, holl ryganau gwyrddion;
Duw a faddau i mi fy meiau,
Mynd sydd raid i ganlyn Angau.

Lads and lasses all, goodbye,
Farewell, verdant fields of rye,
God forgive me my misdeeds,
All must go where'er Death leads.

Pererin wyf

Pererin wyf mewn anial dir,
Yn crwydro yma a thraw,
Ac yn rhyw ddisgwyl bob yr awr
Fod tŷ fy Nhad gerllaw.

Ac mi debygaf clywaf sŵn
Nefolaidd rai o'm blaen,
Wedi gorchfygu a mynd drwy
Dymhestloedd dŵr a thân.

Tyrd, Ysbryd Sanctaidd, ledia'r ffordd,
Bydd imi'n niwl a thân;
Ni cherdda' i'n gywir hanner cam
Oni byddi di o'm blaen.

Mi wyraf weithiau ar y dde
Ac ar yr aswy law;
Am hynny arwain, gam a cham,
Fi i'r baradwys draw.

Mae hiraeth arnaf am y wlad
Lle mae torfeydd di-ri'
Yn canu'r anthem ddyddiau'u hoes
Am angau Calfari.

Pantycelyn, the home of William Williams

I am a pilgrim
William Williams, 18th century

I am a pilgrim wandering
About a desert land,
Expecting hourly to find
My Father's house at hand.

And I do hear the heavenly sound
Of those who went before,
Through storms of flames and water, on
To conquer evermore.

Come, Holy Spirit, lead the way,
And go before my face;
Unless you be my cloud and fire
I'll take not half a pace.

I sometimes veer towards the right
Or to the left instead,
Therefore lead me, step by step,
To Paradise ahead.

I have a longing for the land
Where hosts eternally
And numberless are singing of
The death on Calvary.

The 19th Century

Detectable in the eighteenth century are the emergence of two schools of thought concerning the Welsh language. On the one hand the Romantic, which regarded it as venerable and refined, dating back to a druidical (or biblical) prehistory, and capable of the highest spiritual expression. On the other hand the Utilitarian, which saw it as an antiquated tongue of ignorant peasants, a barrier to progress best deleted or at least discouraged.

Among the Romantics, none was more active or persuasive than Edward Williams (Iolo Morganwg), poet, stonemason and self-taught antiquary. Aided by a fondness of laudanum, he concocted an account of the poetic tradition which claimed that it had descended unbroken from the ancient druids, and that he was the sole remaining inheritor of its secrets. He also produced poems and other testimony supporting this claim, supposedly copied by him from old manuscripts unfortunately unavailable for inspection by others. It says much of his abilities, and the state of nineteenth century scholarship, that his numerous confections remained unchallenged for a century.

To be fair, he wasn't the only one. All over Europe, small nations such as Wales, Scotland and Bohemia were coming under cultural pressure from their stronger neighbours, and one common response was to creatively adjust the past in order to ensure that one's culture could still command at least some respect, if only that due to old age. Such works also appealed strongly to those disenchanted with the rise of industrialism and contemporary urban squalor, preferring to escape, in imagination at least, to a past of green bowers, valiant knights, fair maidens and tuneful minstrels.

To the Utilitarians, this talk of druids and bards merely confirmed the suspicion that Welsh culture had nothing to offer to the modern age, and could be banished to the realm of wishful thinking. Celts, it was argued, were inherently impractical dreamers: but properly trained could become useful workers, or at least soldiers. Their old, easy-going but occasionally violent agricultural way of life had to be displaced: the new industrial age needed a regulated, disciplined, educated workforce, all running to the same timetable, all sharing the same values, all speaking the same language. English, of course. To all practical purposes, the Utilitarians won out.

This wasn't achieved at once, and didn't immediately concern the Welsh poets, though like society in general, the *eisteddfodau* and literary life did become more organized, with a framework of Sunday Schools, penny readings and literary associations promoting literacy and encouraging composition. Given these new opportunities, the creative output of the nineteenth century increased enormously: but unfortunately much of it was diverted to theological squabbles, with a tendency to judge quality by size. Like contemporary sermons, no great poem could be considered complete until it had said absolutely everything about its subject that could be said, and more. The result was reams of ponderous, forgettable, eisteddfodic verse: technically correct, but hopelessly uninspired.

Small wonder that most people preferred the shorter form of the lyric. Like hymns, these compositions were comparatively brief, appealed directly to

the sentiments, and were easily memorized. Although they originated in the older tradition of free verse, they became increasingly popular from the mid-nineteenth century onwards as periodicals and printed anthologies became more affordable, favourite ones being taught and passed from one generation to the next. It's a form which has yet to go out of fashion.

As pressure to conform with British norms increased, the Welsh became more eager to ape their neighbours, and were keenly aware, and responsive to, English public opinion regarding Wales. We adopted a 'shame culture': one which needed alien approbation in order to feel confident of its own intrinsic value, and which took for granted the precedence of English. So much so, that it effectively became a subculture. The Welsh conformed to what was expected of good British citizens, and the National Eisteddfod, held from the 1860s onwards, awarded the first prizes of a chair for strict-metre poetry, and a crown for free-metre poetry. It became an annual showcase of Welsh virtuosity, confirming a self-image of a hard-working, law-

abiding, God-fearing people, for whom poets provided the requisite politically and morally correct verse. Poetry which acted as a powerful vector for that affliction of the Victorian aspiring class, sentimentality.

Not that there wasn't some dissent. Wales, after all, had been a centre of Chartism, and was becoming a stronghold of Liberalism. Ballads protesting about the lot of the poor circulated, and higher up the social scale, *eisteddfodau* began to attract competitors other than poetic preachers. Some cultivated a philosophical, abstract style characterized by obscurity, *sturm und drang*. More, influenced by the same disenchantment with industrialization which gave rise to the Arts and Crafts movement in England, returned to Romanticism, harking back to an idealized medieval past. Sensuous, personal and semi-pagan, it wasn't always inspired (one volume being derided as 'machine-made poetry on hand-made paper'): but its proponents did cast new light on the poetic tradition, promote awareness of the poetry of nations apart from England, and raise the standard of literary criticism.

By the begining of the twentieth century Wales' population was higher than ever, of whom about a million were Welsh-speaking. There was modest prosperity, the standard of living had never been better, and the chapels were full. Progress was assured.

A nineteenth century Eisteddfod at Caernarfon castle

Gofyn cosyn

Moled ereill aml diroedd,
Tai mawrion gwychion ar goedd;
Dogn o aur da gan rywrai,
Digon o rwysg da gan rai;
Gwell yw pleser gan ereill
Na chur a llafur y lleill;
Nwydog win i'w digoni
Ceisio maent, ond caws i mi!
I rai ereill bo'r arian,
Y wledd, a'r rhwysgedd yn rhan;
Ac o Eifion, burion bau,
Menyn a chaws i minnau!

Cwynais, ad-gwynais ganwaith,
Heb fenyn, na chosyn chwaith;
Heb gaws haf yn fy ngafael
'R wy'n adyn di-gosyn gwael,
Heb un hoen – byw anhynaws,
Nych neu gur – O, na chawn gaws!

Ceisiaf gan addfwynaf ddyn,
Ceisiaf gardota cosyn;
A gwir hyn, â'r gŵr hynaws
Dygymydd cywydd y caws;
Gwrendy'r Bardd, ŵr hardd, ar hyn,
Ac er cysur ceir cosyn;
Ni rydd nag, groesnag, grasnaws,
Ond im ar fyr y gyr gaws!

Requesting a cheese
Morris Williams (Nicander), 1809 – 1874

Let others praise a wide estate,
And of fine mansions then relate;
Some do like receiving gold,
Others to pomp and splendour hold;
Some love pleasure, and distain
All the others' toil and pain;
In lusty wine some seek to please
All their cravings – but give me cheese!
To others let the money fall,
The feasting and the grandeur all;
From fair Eifionydd, let there be
Cheese and butter given me!

A hundred times I cried 'alack!',
Still cheese and butter did I lack;
Of summer cheese, I've not a one,
I'm wretched, cheeseless, woebegone,
Joyless, weak and ill at ease:
Life's uncongenial – oh, for cheese!

I'll beg a big-hearted man
For a whole cheese, if I can;
He's affable: the Ode to Cheese
(the truth be told) is sure to please.

Poed in y caws, paid nacàu,
O, rho gosyn rhag eisiau!
Caws braf, caws haf, caws hufen,
Caws brych, caws harddwych, caws hen,
Caws cyfan, caws y cofir
Yn ein hoes am dano'n hir!

To him, fine Poet, will I sing
And get a cheese most comforting.
He'll not refuse ungraciously:
At once, he'll send a cheese to me!

Let there be cheese, and don't hold back,
Give us cheese, lest we suffer lack!
Summer cheese, cheese fine, cheese creamy,
Cheese beautiful, mature and tawny,
A whole cheese, and a cheese to be
Long treasured in our memory!

Caerphilly – home of a famous Welsh cheese

I DIC PENDERYN

GANED RICHARD LEWIS
YM 1808. YN ABERAFAN
CROGWYD yng NGHARCHAR
CAERDYDD ar AWST 13-1831
AR OL Y TERFYSG YM
MERTHYR YR UN FLWYDDYN
MERTHYR GWEITHWYR CYMRU

BORN RICHARD LEWIS
IN 1808 IN ABERAVON
AND HANGED at CARDIFF
GAOL on August 13TH 1831
FOLLOWING THE MERTHYR
INSURRECTION OF THAT YEAR
A MARTYR of THE
WELSH WORKING CLASS

Baled Dic Penderyn (*detholiadau*)

Casglodd naw mil yn lled-afrywiog,
I sefyll allan am fwy o gyflog,
Rhai heb waith a'r lleill yn cwynfan,
A'r bwyd yn ddrud a chyflog fechan...

Hi aeth yn derfysg mawr ym Merthyr,
Gorfod gyrru ffwrdd am filwyr;
Pan ddaeth rhai fyny o Abertawe,
Fe aeth gwŷr Merthyr ffwrdd â'u harfau.

Ond fe ddaeth milwyr o Aberhonddu,
Hi aeth yn rhyfel pan ddaeth y rheini,
Ac fe laddwyd o wŷr Merthyr,
Un ar hugain yn y frwydr...

Bu raid i'r mobs i roddi fyny,
A llawer iawn ga'dd eu carcharu;
Pan ddaeth y Sesiwn, er mawr alaeth,
Fe'u barnwyd oll yn ôl y gyfraith.

Hwy gawsant oll eu bywyd gweddus
I gyd ond un, sef Richard Lewis;
Er cymaint oedd am safio hwnnw,
Ynghrog ar bren efe ga'dd farw...

Dic Penderyn's memorial plaque, St Mary's Street, Cardiff and Castell Cyfarthfa, Merthyr Tydfil – the seat of the Crawshays, the Iron Barons

The ballad of Dic Penderyn (*extracts*)
Richard Williams (*Dic Dywyll*), 1831

Nine thousand then stood out together,
Quite angrily, their wage to better,
Some unemployed, some voicing grievance,
The food so dear, and paid a pittance...

In Merthyr there were great disorders,
So they were forced to send for soldiers;
When Swansea troops obeyed the summons,
Merthyr men then seized their weapons.

But Brecon soldiers then arrived there,
And when they came, all fell to warfare;
Of Merthyr men after the fighting,
Twenty-one lay dead or dying...

Then the mobs capitulated,
Great numbers were incarcerated;
They faced judgement (oh, affliction!)
At the sitting of the Session.

To them all their lives were granted,
Richard Lewis being excepted;
Though so many were for saving
That man's life, he died by hanging...

Rhieingerdd

Dau lygad disglair fel dwy em
Sydd i'm hanwylyd i,
Ond na bu em belydrai 'rioed
Mor fwyn â'i llygad hi.

Am wawr ei gwddf dywedyd wnawn
Mai'r cann claerwynnaf yw,
Ond bod rhyw lewych gwell na gwyn,
Anwylach yn ei liw.

Mae holl dyneraf liwiau'r rhos
Yn hofran ar ei grudd;
Mae'i gwefus fel pe cawsai'i lliw
O waed y grawnwin rhudd.

A chlir felyslais ar ei min
A glywir megis cân
Y gloyw ddŵr yn tincial dros
Y cerrig gwynion mân.

A chain y seinia'r hen Gymraeg
Yn ei hyfrydlais hi;
Mae iaith bereiddia'r ddaear hon
Ar enau 'nghariad i.

Love song
John Morris Jones, 1864 – 1929

My true love, she has two eyes
And like two gems are they;
But they're brighter, brighter still
Than gemstones any day.

About her throat, I'd dare to say
It's white as white could be;
But dearer, better still than that
It's plain enough to see.

The tenderest colours of the rose
Her lovely cheeks do shape
And on her lips resides the dusky
Crimson of the grape.

Her voice is like the tinkling stream
A-singing of its song
As it wends its crystal way
The white-stoned brook along.

How beautiful the mother-tongue
Which from her lips is heard
In my love's voice, it surely is
The sweetest in the world.

'like the tinkling stream'

A synio'r wyf mai sŵn yr iaith,
Wrth lithro dros ei min,
Roes i'w gwefusau'r lluniaidd dro,
A lliw a blas y gwin.

And I do think that language fair
Of this true love of mine
Has formed upon her shapely lips
The tint and taste of wine.

War

The cataclysm of the First World War changed everything. For centuries, War had always been away somewhere else, fought by men who had parted from society and were generally despised as being little better than criminals. Now it had come into every household in the land, mass war, industrial war, demanding, tearing men from their families and communities, subordinating all else. People whose world had revolved around the certainties of workplace and chapel, harvest and annual fair found themselves a few weeks later in the appalling mire of the Western Front or the fly-infested hell of Mesopotamia, killing and dying. It was beyond all previous experience, and they had no vocabulary with which to describe it.

They didn't need to, for the time being, because the Government was doing all the speaking. Once Westminster had set in motion its organs of publicity and propaganda, the poets of Wales joined in the war effort with an enthusiastic outpouring of patriotism and jingoism. They got to grips with such unfamiliar subjects as 'The U-boat' and 'The Sniper', and in newspapers, magazines and books praise was heaped upon Lloyd George, opprobrium on the Kaiser, and young men were urged to go to war, to fight and die gloriously like Llywelyn and Glyndŵr, in order to defend their homeland and protect small countries. The irony of this was unappreciated at the time.

Such purposeful, 'utilitarian' poems were a continuation of the Victorian popular lyrical tradition, peopled with stock images and characters drawn from a picture-postcard image of a sweet, safe, quiet little Wales of Virtuous Mothers, Harps and Whitewashed Cottages. Such poetry as did filter back from the Front Line, and got published, tended to confirm the stereotype. Anti-war poems there were, but these were largely confined to pacifist publications of very limited appeal.

Among the poets was Ellis Humphrey Evans of Trawsfynydd, better known by his bardic pseudonym Hedd Wyn. He responded to the war, initially, as did most others, with patriotic and consolatory verse: but his poem *Rhyfel* ('War') indicates a transformation, a change of view provoked by a sense of weary purposelessness. His entry for the 1917 National Eisteddfod, *Yr Arwr* ('The Hero'), however, was a Romantic glorification of sacrifice as means of return from the chaos of war to a world of peace and virtue. He won first prize: but was killed at the Battle of Passchendaele six weeks before the Eisteddfod, and the chairing ceremony – and the figure of Hedd Wyn himself – was so orchestrated as to channel a cathartic outpouring of national grief, and stoke anti-German feeling, at a politically opportune moment for Lloyd George.

Patriotic poetry continued to be produced after 1918, but there was increasing dissent. Some of the *englynion* now required for war memorials across Wales had about them more grief than glory, and in 1919 W. J. Gruffydd's *1914–1918: Yr Ieuanc wrth yr Hen* ('1914–1918: The Young to the Old') blasted the 'old men' who had sent the young to die. It was in 1921, however, that a real impact was made when Albert Evans-Jones' poem *Mab y Bwthyn* ('The Cottage Lad') won the crown at the National Eisteddfod, though not without a deal of trepidation on the part of the judges. It

Penygroes memorial to young men killed in the war, with an englyn *by R. Williams Parry*

chronicled the journey of a country boy to the battlefield, to post-war London, and finally back to a rural idyll with his beloved: and was firmly in the Romantic style.

What caused dismay were his graphic descriptions of trench warfare, of the off-duty attractions of wine and women, and of loose life in the Empire's capital city. Not that he condoned such things, but the very mention of them was more than enough: this poetry wasn't uplifting,

wasn't nice. His Y *Tannau Coll* ('The Missing Harpstrings') of 1922 contained more of the same, just as his *Balâd Wrth Gofeb y Milwyr* ('Ballade By The Soldiers' Memorial') acidly castigated the hypocrisy of those who shed crocodile tears on Rememberance Day.

The literary establishment counter-attacked. No-one, it was argued, wanted to discuss the War any more: it was all over, and a return should be made to true poetry, free of dirty realism. Evans-Jones himself, who hadn't actually questioned the political, religious and moral *status quo*, eventually retreated to escapism and conformity, but *Mab y Bwthyn*'s style and content made it popular, and it spawned emulators. Further controversy erupted over E. Prosser Rhys' prizewinning poem *Atgof* ('Memory) of 1924, with its references to homosexuality, leading to efforts to clamp down on such poetic deviancy: so although D. Gwenallt Jones' 1928 ode *Y Sant* ('The Saint') was judged winner at the National Eisteddfod that year, it was refused a prize because of its intimations of lust.

It was too late: *Mab y Bwthyn* had opened a door that could not be closed. Gradually, and later than in England, the Welshmen and women of the Great War found the words they had lacked. R. Williams-Parry's tender 1924 *englynion* in memory of Hedd Wyn, and T. Cennech Davies' audacious 1926 poem on the same subject, stand out: and from the 1930s onwards people began to publish about their wartime experiences. Mostly, however, in prose: because for many, the old poetic forms with which they were familiar, the eisteddfodic ode and the romantic lyric, could not express the sheer magnitude and awfulness of what had happened to them, of what had been done.

The Welsh National Monument, Flanders

Baled trychineb Senghennydd
(*rhan*)

Newydd pruddaidd fflachiwyd heddiw
Gan y wifren trwy y tir
Am alaethus, farwol ddamwain
Edy ôl am amser hir;
Llawer mam a hoffus briod,
Ieuainc blant o bob ryw radd,
A alarant am anwyliaid –
Yn y glô-bwll wedi 'u lladd!

Yn Morgannwg bu y danchwa,
Yn Senghennydd, ger Caerdydd,
Enw eilw prudd adgofion
Am ffrwydriadau eraill sydd
Wedi digwydd yn y llecyn, –
Chwerw yw eu côf o hyd –
Rhandir enwog am ei mwnau
A anfonir dros y byd.

Roedd naw cant o'r gweithwyr druain
Wrth eu gorchwyl wyth o'r gloch,
Pan y clywid trwy yr ardal
Sŵn a welwai lawer boch:

The ballad of the Senghennydd disaster (*extract*)
Anonymous, 1913

Dismal news today came flashing
Throughout the land over the wire,
Of an accident long-lasting
In effect, fatal and dire.
Many loving wives and mothers,
Infants well and lowly bred,
Are now mourning for their dear ones,
In the coalmine lying dead!

An explosion at Senghennydd,
In Glamorgan brings to mind
Memories of detonations,
Sad to say, of similar kind
Which have happened in that area –
Oh, so bitter to recall –
Famous for its ore exported
Across the world to one and all.

Nine hundred of these poor workers
By eight o'clock were at the site,
When was heard throughout the area
A sound at which the cheeks turned white:

Ergyd greodd ofn a dychryn,
Ddygodd bang i lawer bron,
Ac ar fyrder rhuthrodd cannoedd
At y Pwll lle deuai hon.

Poen a phryder lanwai mynwes
Pawb oedd yno, bach a mawr;
Ofnid mai lladdedig pob-dyn
O'r naw canwr oedd i lawr,
Ac roedd cofio tanchwa arall
A ddigwyddodd yn 'run fan,
Pan y lladdwyd pawb ond un-dyn,
Yn lladd gobaith oedd ond gwan.

Trwm arswydol oedd yr ergyd,
A distrywiol ym mhob modd:
Pen y pwll ddioddefodd effaith
Canlyniadau erch a rodd;
Yno lladdwyd dyn anffodus
Safai ugain llath o'r fan,
Ei ben chwythwyd mewn amrantiad –
Ei gorph a gafwyd yn ddau ran...

A thunderclap of fear and horror
Brought to many breasts a pain,
Sending hundreds quickly running
To the Pit from whence it came.

In the breasts of all there present,
Great and small, did terror grow,
Fear that Death had claimed the lives of
All nine hundred down below.
Memories of an explosion
At that same place, to recall,
In which all but one man perished,
Killed a hope already small.

So tremendous an explosion,
All-destructive in effect,
Its appalling consequences
Left the pit-head but a wreck.
There was slain a man ill-fated,
Standing twenty yards away,
His head blown off in an instant,
His body in two pieces lay...

Dymuniad

Dymunwn fod yn flodyn – a'r awel
Garuaidd yn disgyn
Arnaf i yn genlli gwyn
Oddi ar foelydd eurfelyn.

A wish

Ellis Humphrey Evans (Hedd Wyn), 1887 – 1917

I'd wish to be a flower – and caressed
By a breeze so tender
From golden hills, to confer
On me a shining shower.

Atgof

Dim ond lleuad borffor
Ar fin y mynydd llwm,
A sŵn hen afon Prysor
Yn canu yn y cwm.

A memory

Nought but a purple moon
Above the moorland hung,
As in the glen old Prysor goes
Singing as it flows along.

A full moon above the Rhinogydd, Trawsfynydd

Y blotyn du

Nid oes gennym hawl ar y sêr,
Na'r lleuad hiraethus chwaith,
Na'r cwmwl o aur a ymylch
Yng nghanol y glesni maith.

Nid oes gennym hawl ar ddim byd
Ond ar yr hen ddaear wyw;
A honno sy'n anhrefn i gyd
Yng nghanol gogoniant Duw.

The black spot

We haven't a claim on the stars,
Nor on the lonesome moon,
Nor on the golden cloud that bathes
Amidst the unbounded blue.

We haven't a claim in the world,
There's nothing that's yours or mine,
But the dear old earth, all gone to rack
Amidst the glory Divine.

Gorffen crwydro

Ceraist ti grwydro gwledydd pellennig,
Y gwledydd sy 'mhell tros y don;
Weithiau dychwelit i'th gartre mynyddig
A'th galon yn ysgafn a llon.

Gwelsom di ennyd cyn dychwel ohonot
I'r rhyfel sy'n crynu y byd;
Nodau y gwlatgar a'r beiddgar oedd ynot,
Y nodau sy'n costio mor ddrud.

Fe chwyth y corwynt tros fryniau Trawsfynydd
O'th ôl fel yn athrist ei gainc
Tithau yng nghwmni'r fataliwn ddihysbydd
Sy'n cysgu'n ddifreuddwyd yn Ffrainc.

An end to roaming

You loved to roam the distant lands,
The countries beyond the sea,
Sometimes you'd return to your highland home,
And so light of heart you'd be.

We saw you awhile before you returned
To the war that makes the world quake,
Bearing the marks so dearly bought
For your country and bravery's sake.

The storm rages over Trawsfynydd's hills
After you, as if it would weep;
You, who with numberless battalions in France
Lie there in a dreamless sleep.

Rhyfel

Gwae fi fy myw mewn oes mor ddreng,
A Duw ar drai ar orwel pell;
O'i ôl mae dyn, yn deyrn a gwreng,
Yn codi ei awdurdod hell.

Pan deimlodd fyned ymaith Dduw
Cyfododd gledd i ladd ei frawd;
Mae sŵn yr ymladd ar ein clyw,
A'i gysgod ar fythynnod tlawd.

Mae'r hen delynau genid gynt
Ynghrog ar gangau'r helyg draw,
A gwaedd y bechgyn lond y gwynt,
A'u gwaed yn gymysg efo'r glaw.

War

Woe that I live at this fell time,
When God has ebbed so far away;
And man into His place did climb,
Both king and churl, to demand sway.

When he felt God no longer near,
He raised the killing sword aloft:
The sound of battle fills the ear,
Its shadow's on the poor man's croft.

The ancient harps which once were played
Now hang on willows over there,
And in the rain boys' blood is made
To flow; their screaming fills the air.

Englynion coffa Hedd Wyn (*rhan*)

Y bardd trwm dan bridd tramor, — y dwylo
  Na ddidolir rhagor:
   Y llygaid dwys dan ddwys ddôr,
   Y llygaid na all agor.

Wedi ei fyw y mae dy fywyd, — dy rawd
  Wedi ei rhedeg hefyd:
   Daeth awr i fynd i'th weryd,
   A daeth i ben deithio byd.

Tyner yw'r lleuad heno — tros fawnog
  Trawsfynydd yn dringo:
   Tithau'n drist a than dy ro
   Ger y ffos ddu'n gorffwyso.

Trawsfynydd! Tros ei feini — trafaeliaist
  Ar foelydd Eryri:
   Troedio wnest ei rhedyn hi,
   Hunaist ymhell ohoni.

The elegy for Hedd Wyn (*extract*)
R. Williams Parry, 1884 – 1956

The laureate who lies buried – abroad,
  The hands forever tied;
   The sad eyes deeply covered,
   The eyes now forever closed.

For your life has now been lived – and your span
  Came be to completed.
   Now's the hour: in earth you're laid,
   Your travels terminated.

Tender the moon this evening – as above
  Trawsfynydd it's rising;
   You so sad, as you lie in
   The black trench of your resting.

Trawsfynydd! From its stony, – bare peatlands
  You wandered Eryri;
   You walked your brackened country,
   Now you sleep so distantly.

Aftermath

The profound social, spiritual and political changes in Wales following the War were reflected in a new kind of poetry, broadly labelled 'Modernism'. Already hinted at in T. H. Parry-Williams' 1915 'Y Ddinas' ('The City'), this was the antithesis of Romanticism: it was cynical, realistic, vernacular to the point of slanginess, and employed new free-metre forms, including vers libre. Its subjects were concrete, and it attempted, above all, to make sense of a Wales in which the old certainties had been blasted away, and people were left scrabbling amidst the wreckage for explanations and answers. How had they been so hoodwinked and manipulated? Why were the same moral bankrupts still in charge? How had the rich profited, while yesterday's heroes were now on the dole?

The Empire was foundering, and Wales was in danger of going down with it. Chapel attendance, population levels and the percentage of people able to speak Welsh were declining, and the Welsh economy was depressed. Retreat to sweet Romantic despair was not an option in the face of crisis and existential anguish which demanded a far more profound response. Marxism had its attractions, but in practice left many disillusioned. The present was chaotic, and nothing could be drawn from an unknown future: so by the 1930s many of the modernists had turned to look anew at the only available source of inspiration, the past. Not a past of romantic fantasy, but that of an independent, warrior nation of deep Christian tradition, far deeper than the smug, trite pieties of the nineteenth century, far removed from contemprary compromise and materialism.

Not that there weren't other voices. Sentimental lyricism still sold best, but in other poets Romanticism developed in new directions, towards an interest in psychology and the innermost recesses of the subconscious, or a renewed celebration of the simpler, rural life of tradition and craftsmanship. Others derided such tendencies, challenging the poets to face up to the challenge of the modern world. Modernists were also perceived to be academic elitists, producers of 'food for giraffes' rather than songs for ordinary folk.

The Welsh Nationalist Party, Plaid

Cymru, had been formed in 1925, and in 1936 three prominent members – and poets – took direct action by burning down some buildings at an aircraft bombing range. This and subsequent events galvanized Welsh poetry for decades afterwards, as nationalism took hold as a real political and cultural force. Wales' crisis was seen to be not merely one of economics or administration, but of the nation's very existence, relentlessly eroded by an increasing English-dominated centralism which made Welsh language and culture marginalized and irrelevant. The poets responded as they had not done since the days of Owain Glyndŵr, by becoming warriors and prophets once more.

This wave was muted, but not stopped, by the Second World War. Indeed it's arguable that of the two events, 1936 left much the greater mark on Welsh poetry. Having been traumatized by the First World War, 1939 found a people already innured to mass conflict, and who had yet to fully digest that experience. The Second World War, for all its trauma, was but an aftershock, and its lasting impact was not fully felt until years afterwards, as the shadows of Belsen and Hiroshima deepened on all of Western civilization. How, it was asked, could there be any poetry, any art at all, after such deeds? How could such horrors be comprehended or expressed? What relevance, now, had tinkering about with alliteration and rhyme?

Yet the poet has to sing or suffocate, and however much some may have been tempted to despair, Wales had its own continuing struggle, and poetry continued to be produced along the theme already determined before the War: the survival of Christian, Welsh-speaking civilization, even in the face of popular apathy, official hostility and the threat of nuclear annihilation. More so, as the threat to the existence of Welsh culture was becoming increasingly obvious. Matters came to a head with the drowning of a Welsh-speaking community in 1965 in order to provide a water supply for Liverpool.

This was an era of protest and direct action all over the world, and in Wales it took the form of mass campaigns to safeguard what was left of Welsh-speaking communities, and promote the use of the Welsh language. A new generation of poets

took up this challenge, foremost among them being Gerallt Lloyd Owen, Alan Llwyd and Dic Jones. Far from abandoning the strict-metre tradition, they reinvigorated it with so much fresh energy that it flourishes still.

But for how long? The nationalist movement has arguably lost steam since the 1980s, and the decline in the percentage of Welsh-speakers and, crucially, the number of Welsh-speaking communities, continues. That many poets have now turned from national survival to other themes of more personal and individual interest could be interpreted as increased confidence in the present and future, or as an abandonment of the struggle in the absence of any real success: '...and Israel was smitten, and they fled every man into his tent.' The same could be said about the trend for some Welsh-speaking poets to compose in English: necessary outreach, or throwing in the towel? Further, there has been a loss of that spiritual continuity which has characterized and energized Welsh culture since its beginnings. Many of the new generation have little concept of belief, and regard religion as a set of absurd moral restrictions tending to incite its followers to violence against others.

There are, for the moment, an encouraging number of young and gifted Welsh poets of both sexes: but the Welsh ship is plainly low in the water. The tradition has survived thus far by transmission from one generation, one social group to another: but always in the context of the Welsh-speaking community, of a whole society with a common language and values, as opposed to atomized individuals. If that's lost, then there's no other place to go, no other vessel in sight. The ship will finally have sunk, and the poetic tradition along with it.

A slogan etched into Welsh memory. The community of Capel Celyn in the Tryweryn valley was drowned to provide water for Liverpool.

Mab y bwthyn (*rhannau*)

Yr oedd mynd ar y jazz-band,
a mynd ar y ddawns,
A mynd ar y byrddau
lle'r oedd chwarae siawns;
Yr oedd mynd ar y gwirod
a mynd ar y gwin
A mynd ar y tango,
lin wrth lin,
Yr oedd mynd ar y chwerthin,
a mynd ar y gân,
A'r sŵn fel clindarddach
drain ar dân...

Euthum i wersyll ger y dref
Lle codai gwŷr di Dduw eu llef,
Gwŷr a gyfarthai megis cŵn:
Yno trwy fryntni oer, a sŵn,
A darostyngiad o bob gradd,
Fe'm gwnaethant i
yn beiriant lladd;
Ac yn fy llaw rhoddasant wn,
Ac ar fy nghefn
rhwymasant bwn,
Ac anfonasant fi i'r gad
'I ymladd dros iawnderau 'ngwlad.'...

Rhywbryd rhwng un o'r gloch a dau
Yr oeddem drwy'r mieri'n gwau
Yn ôl drachefn am yr hen ffos
Lle safem neithiwr gyda'r nos;
Yn ôl dros ddaear llithrig wleb

The cottage lad (*extracts*)
Albert Evans-Jones (**Cynan**), 1895 – 1970

The jazz was hot, the crowds swung to the dance,
They pressed about tables of games of chance,
There were wines and spirits in flowing supply,
And they danced the tango, thigh to thigh,
The laughter and singing went higher and higher,
Like the noise of the crackling of thorns in a fire...

I went to a barracks by the town,
Where godless men did bawl and frown,
Men who barked like curs at boys,
Who by brutality and noise
And degradation, by degree,
Made a killer out of me;
And they gave me a gun and pack
In my hand and on my back,
And then they sent me off to fight
'To defend my country's right.'...

Sometime between one and two
We made our way through brambles to
The same old trench, where the previous night
We'd stood and waited for the fight;
Back across what was No Man's Land,
Over the wet and slippery earth, and

Y fan a fu yn Rhandir Neb;
O dan y gwifrau-pigog, geirwon,
A thros bentyrrau hen o'r meirwon.
O Dduw! a raid im gofio sawr
Y fan lle'r heidiai'r llygod mawr,
A bysedd glas *y pethau mud*
Ar glic eu gynnau bron i gyd?...

Under the barbed wire's talons, ahead
Of climbing heaps of the long-since-dead.
Oh, God! must I recall the reek
Of that place where the rats swarmed sleek
And those *mute things*' rotting fingers
All frozen on their rifles' triggers?...

Gras cyn bwyd

O Dad, yn deulu dedwydd – y deuwn
 Â diolch o'r newydd;
 Cans o'th law y daw bob dydd
 Ein lluniaeth a'n llawenydd.

Grace before a meal
W. D. Williams, 1900 – 1985

Father, as a family – we anew
 Give thanks most happily;
 For to us, there comes daily
 Joy and sustenance from thee.

Hwiangerddi (*rhan*)

Arglwydd, gad im bellach gysgu,
Trosi'r wyf ers oriau du:
Y mae f'enaid yn terfysgu
A ffrwydradau ar bob tu.

O! na ddeuai chwa i'm suo
O Garn Fadryn ddistaw, bell,
Fel na chlywn y gynnau'n rhuo
Ond gwrando am gân y dyddiau gwell...

Lullabies (*extract*)
Albert Evans-Jones (**Cynan**), 1895 – 1970

Lord! now let me sleep a moment,
Darkness brings no rest at all,
For my soul is in such torment
As all around me bombshells fall.

Oh! for just a breeze to lull me
From Carn Fadryn's quiet ways,
Shutting out the guns about me,
And bearing songs of better days...

Tresaith

Beth sydd i'w weled yn Nhresaith
Ym min yr hwyr, ym min yr hwyr?
Yr eigion euog a'i fron yn llaith
Yn troi a throsi mewn hunllef faith;
A hyn sydd i'w weled yn Nhresaith.

Beth sydd i'w glywed yn Nhresaith
Ym min yr hwyr, ym min yr hwyr?
Cri gwylan unig â'i bron dan graith
Yn dyfod yn ôl o seithug daith;
A hyn sydd i'w glywed yn Nhresaith.

Beth sydd i'w deimlo yn Nhresaith
Ym min yr hwyr, ym min yr hwyr?
Calon alarus, â'i hiraeth maith
Yn sŵn y tonnau yn caffael iaith;
A hyn sydd i'w deimlo yn Nhresaith.

Tresaith

Tresaith

What's to be seen here in Tresaith
As dusk comes down, as dusk comes down?
The guilty ocean's watery breast
Long in nightmarish unrest;
That's to be seen here in Tresaith.

What's to be heard here in Tresaith
As dusk comes down, as dusk comes down?
A lonely seagull's cry of pain
Having voyaged all in vain;
That's to be heard here in Tresaith.

What's to be felt here in Tresaith
As dusk comes down, as dusk comes down?
A grieving heart, in yearning long,
By the waves' sound given tongue;
That's to be felt here in Tresaith.

Y Grib Goch

Gwaedda –
ni chynhyrfi braidd y llethrau hyn,
rhaeadr y defaid maen,
y panig di-frys, di-fref,
y rhuthr pendramwnwgl, stond:
a fugeiliodd mynyddoedd ia,
a wlanodd rhew ac eira a niwl,
a gneifiodd corwynt a storm
yng nglas y byd –
ni ddychryni'r rhain.

Gwaedda – tafl dy raff
(oni chipia'r gwynt dy edau o lais)
fil o droedfeddi crog
am gyrn y tarw-wyll sy â'i aruthr dwlc
rhyngot a'r dydd.

Gwaedda –
Ni thâl geiriau yma:
onid ddoe y ganwyd hwy,
y baban-glebrwyd hwy
mewn ogof fan draw?

Crib Goch
T. Rowland Hughes, 1903 – 1949

Shout –
you won't alarm these slopes' flock,
the torrent of stone sheep,
the static, silent panic,
the frozen stampede:
shepherded by glaciers,
bewoolled by ice and snow and mist,
shorn by tempest and storm
at the dawn of the world –
you won't scare these.

Shout – cast your rope
(unless the wind should snatch away your
threadlike voice)
a thousand dangling feet
about the horns of that awful, bovine brow
which rears between you and the daylight.

Shout –
Words count for nothing here:
weren't they but yesterday born,
yesterday burbled
in yonder cave?

Eifionydd

O olwg hagrwch Cynnydd
Ar wyneb trist y Gwaith
Mae bro rhwng môr a mynydd
Heb arni staen na chraith
Ond lle bu'r arad' ar y ffridd
Yn rhwygo'r gwanwyn pêr o'r pridd.

Draw o ymryson ynfyd
Chwerw'r newyddfyd blin,
Mae yno flas y cynfyd
Yn aros fel hen win.
Hen, hen yw murmur llawer man
Sydd rhwng dwy afon yn Rhos Lan.

A llonydd gorffenedig
Yw llonydd y Lôn Goed
O fwa'i tho plethedig
I'w glaslawr dan fy nhroed.
I lan na thref nid arwain ddim
Ond hynny nid yw ofid im.

O! mwyn yw cyrraedd canol
Y tawel gwmwd hwn
O'm dyffryn diwydiannol
A dull y byd a wn;
A rhodio'i heddwch wrthyf f'hun,
Neu gydag enaid hoff, cytûn.

Eifionydd

R. Williams Parry, 1884 – 1956

Away from where ugly Progress
Makes sad the Quarry's face,
There lies 'tween sea and mountain
A stainless, spotless place,
Save for where the ploughman's toil
Has ripped fair springtime from the soil.

Far from the mad contention
Of this bitter, angry time,
There, the taste of days of yore
Lingers like vintage wine:
And at Rhos Lan, between two rills,
The ancient places murmur still.

In quietude, the wooded lane
Is quietude complete,
From its arching, woven roof
To the grass beneath my feet:
And though it leads not anywhere,
Not church nor township, I don't care.

Oh, how lovely to be in
This place where time runs slow,
Away from my industrial vale,
The world whose ways I know.
Alone its peacefulness I'd stroll,
Or with a favourite, kindred soul.

Y Lôn Goed, Eifionydd (lôn: *lane*; goed: *wooded*)

Hon

Beth yw'r ots gennyf i am Gymru? Damwain a hap
Yw fy mod yn ei libart yn byw. Nid yw hon ar fap

Yn ddim byd ond cilcyn o ddaear mewn cilfach gefn,
Ac yn dipyn o boendod i'r rhai sy'n credu mewn trefn.

A phwy sy'n trigo'n y fangre, dwedwch i mi.
Pwy ond gwehilion o boblach? Peidiwch, da chwi

Â chlegar am uned a chenedl a gwlad o hyd:
Mae digon o'r rhain, heb Gymru, i'w cael yn y byd.

Rwyf wedi alaru ers talm ar glywed grŵn
Y Cymry bondigrybwyll, yn cadw sŵn.

Mi af am dro, i osgoi eu lleferydd a'u llên,
Yn ôl i'm cynefin gynt, a'm dychymyg yn drên.

A dyma fi yno. Diolch am fod ar goll
Ymhell o gyffro geiriau'r eithafwyr oll.

Dyma'r Wyddfa a'i chriw; dyma lymder a moelni'r tir;
Dyma'r llyn a'r afon a'r clogwyn; ac, ar fy ngwir,

Dacw'r tŷ lle'm ganed. Ond wele, rhwng llawr a ne'
Mae lleisiau a drychiolaethau ar hyd y lle.

Rwy'n dechrau simsanu braidd; ac meddaf i chwi,
Mae rhyw ysictod fel petai'n dod drosof i;

Ac mi glywaf grafangau Cymru'n dirdynnu fy mron.
Duw a'm gwaredo, ni allaf ddianc rhag hon.

Her

T. H. Parry-Williams, 1887 – 1975

What care I for Wales? It's but by chance
That I live on her plot of land. Take a glance

At a map: she's but a molehill in some back yard,
And a bit of a nuisance for those who have regard

For order. And tell me now, who lives there?
Who but some common rabble? No, please do spare

Me your spiel about nation and country: of which there's more
Than enough in the world – don't add Wales to that score.

I'm long fed up of hearing the endless drone
Of those (dare I say it) Welshmen who will moan.

I'll take a trainride back down Memory Lane,
To avoid their prattle and print, and go home again.

And now I've arrived, thankfully out of reach
Of all those extremists and their inciting speech.

Here are the mountains, here's the land all barren and bare,
Here's the lake, the river, and the scarp and, I declare,

There's my childhood home: but see, between earth and sky,
Everywhere, there are voices, and spectres, and I'm

Starting to feel a bit queasy, and some malady,
I tell you, is begining to come over me:

And in my breast, I feel her claws dig and scrape:
From Wales, God help me, for me there's no escape.

Y ci defaid

Rhwydd gamwr hawdd ei gymell – i'r mynydd
A'r mannau anghysbell;
Hel a didol diadell
Yw camp hwn yn y cwm pell.

The sheepdog
Thomas Richards, 1883 – 1958

Lithe of step, and easily – persuaded
To pursue at lonely
Shielings; at herding he
Excells in the far valley.

'Here are the mountains'

Preseli

Mur fy mebyd, Foel Drigarn, Carn Gyfrwy, Tal Mynydd,
Wrth fy nghefn ym mhob annibyniaeth barn.
A'm llawr o'r Witwg i'r Wern ac i lawr i'r Efail
Lle tasgodd y gwreichion sydd yn hŷn na harn.

Ac ar glosydd, ar aelwydydd fy mhobl –
Hil y gwynt a'r glaw a'r niwl a'r gelaets a'r grug,
Yn ymgodymu â daear ac wybren ac yn cario
Ac yn estyn yr haul i'r plant, o'u plyg.

Cof ac arwydd, medel ar lethr eu cymydog.
Pedair gwanaf o'r ceirch yn cwympo i'w cais,
Ac un cwrs cyflym, ac wrth laesu eu cefnau
Chwarddiad cawraidd i'r cwmwl, un llef pedwar llais.

Fy Nghymru, a bro brawdoliaeth, fy nghri, fy nghrefydd,
Unig falm i fyd, ei chenhadaeth, ei her,
Perl yr anfeidrol awr yn wystl gan amser,
Gobaith yr yrfa faith ar y drofa fer.

Hon oedd fy ffenestr, y cynaeafu a'r cneifio.
Mi welais drefn yn fy mhalas draw.
Mae rhu, mae rhaib drwy'r fforest ddiffenestr.
Cadwn y mur rhag y bwystfil, cadwn y ffynnon rhag y baw.

Preseli

Waldo Williams, 1904 – 1971

Rampart of my boyhood, Foel Drigarn, Carn Gyfrwy, Tal Mynydd,
There at my back in all independence of thought,
And my ground from Witwg to Wern, and down to the Smithy,
Where flew the sparks since long before iron was wrought.

And on farmyards, on the hearths of my people –
They who with wind, rain and mist, flag and heather are one,
Wrestling with sky and earth, and carrying,
And though bowed, reaching out to pass to the children the sun.

Sign and memory, reaping on their neighbour's brae,
Four swathes of oats falling to them at each try,
And one swift course, and with their backs relaxing
One giant laugh to the clouds, four voices in one cry.

My Wales, and land of brotherhood, my cry, my creed,
The world's only balm, its mission and challenge too,
Pearl of the immortal hour, given by time as a pledge,
Hope, at the shorter turn, for the longer view.

This was my window, the harvesting and shearing.
Over there, in my palace, I saw all in order dwell.
There's a roar, there's rapine throughout the windowless forest.
Let's keep the rampart against the beast, let's keep the filth from the well.

Y mae profion

Y mae profion ein dyddiau ni
Yn awgrymu inni
Ein bod ni –
Bob un wàn jàc ohonom –
Yn diffodd, yn darfod,
Yn peidio â bodoli.

Ond beth am y pethau hynny
O'r ochor draw i angau –
yn furmuron a drychiolaethau –
A lwyddodd, rywfodd,
Trwy oesau bodolaeth dyn
I osgoi gosodiadau awdurdodol,
A dyfarniadau rhesymol,
Gwyddonol, terfynol?

A beth am y llewyrchiadau hynny
O oleuni arallfydol
Sydd y tu hwnt i unrhyw
Ffenomenon naturiol?

A beth am y pethau hynny
Sy'n cyfodi, cyfodi'n dragwyddol
O ofni a rhyfeddu?

Experiments
Gwyn Thomas, 1936 – 2016

Contemporary experiments
Suggest that we –
Every last one of us –
Are being extinguished, dwindling away,
Ceasing to be.

But what about those things
From the other side of dying –
Murmurings and spectres –
Which have succeeded, somehow,
Through the aeons of mankind's existence
To avoid the authoritative pronouncements,
And the reasonable, scientific,
Final judgements?

And what of those glimmerings
Of otherworldly light
Which are beyond any
Natural phenomenon?

And what of those things
That arise, arise eternally
From fear and wondering?

Chwilio

(*Yr ast, wedi boddi ei chŵn bach.*)

Chwilio, heb gael ei cholwyn
Yn y gwellt, a mynych gŵyn.
Un sŵn mwy nid oes yno,
Chwaith na'i gwynfan egwan o.

O'i galar ni fyn aros, -
Ffroeni tyllau cloddiau'r clôs,
O fan i fan, i fyny
I dŷ'r tarw, o'r ffald i'r tŷ.

Rhed yn syn a thyn ei thor
Heibio i ddrws y sgubor,
Ac oedi'n ysig wedyn
O fewn llath i fin y llyn.

Searching
Richard Lewis Jones (**Dic Jones**)*, 1934 – 2009*

(*The bitch, her pups having been drowned.*)

In the straw, she's vainly searching
for her puppy, often whining.
There's no sound there any more,
not a whimper as before.

In her grief, she will not stay,
but goes sniffing on her way:
holes in the farmyard hedge, then higher
up to the fold, the house, the byre.

Passing the barn door, aghast,
tense of belly, running fast,
right up to the pond-side: then
she pauses, and stands broken.

Yr hen gapel, wedi'i werthu i Sais

'Fe'i try yn fwyty,' yw'r farn; – 'o rhoddir
Trwydded, fe'i gwna'n dafarn'.
Mae'n hen adeilad cadarn,
Seiliau ein ffydd sydd yn sarn.

The old chapel, sold to an Englishman
T. Llew Jones, 1915 – 2009

'He'll make it pub, you'll see – if licenced:
Or a diner, maybe'.
The building's strong as can be:
It's our faith that's gone shaky.

Englyn coffa Ellis John Roberts

Wrth glywed yr ehedydd – â'i fyw gân
Cofia, gu ddarllenydd,
Mai Ellis John is hon sydd
Gŵr y miwsig a'r meysydd.

In memory of Ellis John Roberts
John Rowlands, 1911 – 1969

As you hear the lark's timbre – bear in mind
Ellis John, dear reader,
Whom beneath we did inter:
Meadow and music lover.

Carnguwch, Llŷn, where the above epitaph can be seen

Moliant i'r glöwr (rhannau)

Caner, a rhodder iddo – glod dibrin
    Y werin a'i caro;
     Nydder y mawl a haeddo
     I arwr glew erwau'r glo.

Hoenus ddynion sydd yno, – â'u harfau
    Durfin yn morthwylio;
     Dewraf fyddin ddidaro
     Yn glwm wrth y talcen glo.

Isel hur, trwm seguryd – a gofal
    A gafodd, a blinfyd;
     Dwyn beichiau heb wenau byd
     Mewn cell ddu fu ei fywyd.

Dysg yn y talcen am hwyl a phenyd,
Am awr afiaith, a chamwri hefyd,
Y meini afrwydd, a'r cwmni hyfryd,
Hynodrwydd gwŷr, a chaledrwydd gweryd,
A rhin gwerin a'i gwryd – yn troi bro
Y llwch a'r manlo yn wenfro unfryd.

The collier (extracts)
Gwilym Richard Tilsley (Tilsli), 1911 – 1997

Sing, and let him be given – fullsome praise,
    by his loving bretheren;
    let his acclaim be woven,
    hero among mining men.

Down there, a patient army – of brave men
    wielding tools are lively;
    glued to the coalface, they
    with their steel hammer sharply.

Bereft of encouragement – and bowed down
    by much care and torment,
    low pay, and unemployment,
    his life in a dark cell spent.

He learns at the face of fun and contrition,
of sharpness of wit, and of oppression,
of tough rock, and good association,
of the earth's hardness, and men's distinction,
how folks' virtue and action – turn the land
of dust and coal into a radiant region.

*Graveyard gates in Cwm Gwendraeth, remembering the colliers
and quoting a line from this ode*

Fy ngwlad

Wylit, wylit, Lywelyn
Wylit waed pe gwelit hyn.
Ein calon gan estron ŵr,
Ein coron gan goncwerwr
A gwerin o ffafrgarwyr
Llariaidd eu gwên lle'r oedd gwŷr.

Fe rown wên i'r Frenhiniaeth,
Nid gwerin nad gwerin gaeth.
Byddwn daeog ddiogel
A dedwydd iawn, doed a ddêl,
Heb wraidd na chadwynau bro,
Heb ofal ond bihafio.

Ni'n twyllir yn hir gan au
Hanesion rhyw hen oesau.
Y ni o gymedrol nwyd
Yw'r dynion a Brydeiniwyd,
Ni yw'r claear wladgarwyr,
Eithafol ryngwladol wŷr.

Fy ngwlad, fy ngwlad, cei fy nghledd
Yn wridog dros d'anrhydedd.
O gallwn, gallwn golli
Y gwaed hwn o'th blegid di.

My country
Gerallt Lloyd Owen, 1944 – 2014

Oh Llywelyn, thou wouldst weep,
Bloody tears thine eyes would seep,
To see us by a stranger led,
Our crown upon a foreign head,
And those who fought so manfully
Now blithely grin and bend the knee.

We'll smile at all the Royalty,
As servile as but serfs can be;
We'll bow and scrape to save our hides,
And happy be, whate'r betides.
A rootless lot, no longer slave
To old attachments: we'll behave.

As for the past, it's all old hat,
We shan't be long deceived by that.
Now we're men of lukewarm blood,
And of Britannia's brotherhood.
Though patriots, in us you'll see
Extreme impartiality.

My land, my homeland, thou shalt claim
My blushing sword for thy good name,
And I could shed most willingly
All this my very blood for thee.

Dau lygad ar yr un wlad

Rwyt ti'n gweld y tir yn wyllt;
i mi, mae'n ardd erioed.
Fflamau a thân a deimli di;
minnau'n teimlo'r coed.

Cig a weli 'lawr ffroen dy wn;
gwelaf innau gnawd.
Croen a ffwr yn dy feddwl di,
yn fy meddwl innau: brawd.

Rwyt ti'n gweld erwau o wenith gwyn
a minnau'n gweld y paith.
Rwyt ti'n clywed udo yn y nos;
minnau'n clywed iaith.

Rwyt ti'n gweld argae a phibelli dŵr;
minnau'n gweld afon fyw.
Rwyt ti'n cyfri'r lle yn ddarnau aur;
minnau'n ei gyfri'n dduw.

Rwyt ti'n gweld y ddinas yn tyfu o hyd;
rwyf innau'n gweld y ddôl.
Rwyt ti'n gweld cynnydd; minnau'n gweld
y ddaear na ddaw'n ôl.

Two views on the same land
Myrddin ap Dafydd, 1956 –

You see the land a wilderness;
to me, it's fertile ground.
All you feel is fire and flames;
I feel the trees around.

You see meat in your gun's sights;
I see living things.
Hides and furs are on your mind;
and I think: my siblings.

You see endless acres of wheat,
but prairie do I see.
You hear howling in the dark
which sounds like speech to me.

You see dams and drainage pipes;
I see the waters shine.
You count it all in terms of gold;
I count it all divine.

You see a city grow and spread;
the grasslands I discern.
You see progress: I see earth
which never will return.

Taid

'Mae'r helmed hon yn drom, Taid,
mae'n rhaid bod eich pen yn galed a'ch sgwyddau'n llydan:
a phwy fu'n pwytho y faner, Taid?

yn trwsio rhwygiadau'r blynyddoedd
a gwau arian yn nhân y ddraig:
lle gawsoch chi dolc yn y darian, Taid?

a fyddwch chi'n deffro yn chwys oer weithiau,
yn cofio gwaywffon yn hollti,
neu sŵn saeth yn sibrwd wrth drywanu'r awel?

ai dyna pam 'dach chi'n methu cysgu?
a ga'i chwarae â'ch cleddyf, Taid,
ei chodi'n uchel a chyhoeddi heddwch?"

*'Faint yw eich oed chi heddiw, Taid,
a'r bobl o bell yn dwyn cardiau a chyfarchion?'*

'Dwi'n rhy hen, fachgen, i orchymyn, paid!

os llwyddi di ei thynnu o'i gwain ystyfnig
fe gei di gyhoeddi llond gwlad o heddwch
a llunio o'r newydd dy genedl dy hunan.'

*A memorial statue to Wales' national
hero at Corwen, from where he ignited
the revolt of 1400 – 1415*

Grandad

Iwan Llwyd, 1957 – 2010

'This helmet's heavy, Grandad,
  your head must be hard, and your shoulders wide:
  and who stitched the banner, Grandad?

  repairing the rents of the years
  and weaving silver into the dragon's fire:
  where did you get the dent in the shield, Grandad?

  do you sometimes wake in a cold sweat,
  remembering the spear splitting,
  or the hiss of an arrow as it stabs the air?

  is that why you can't sleep?
  and can I play with your sword, Grandad,
  raise it on high and announce peace?'

*'How old are you today, Grandad,
  with the people from afar bearing cards and greetings?'*

'I'm too old, lad, to command, don't!

      if you succeed in drawing it from its stubborn sheath
      you can announce peace throughout the land
      and create anew your own nation.'

P'oni wenwch?

Mae'r gwynt a'r glaw wedi peidio,
mae'r sêr wedi neidio'n ôl,
mae Ab Yr Ynad wedi cael sioc:–
trôdd galar yn *rock 'n roll*.

Mae'r holl ddyniadon fu'n ynfyd
i gyd wedi troi yn gall;
mae'r tir a'r môr yn ôl yn eu lle
yn lle bod y naill yn lle'r llall.

O'r diwedd stopiodd y deri
â pheri twrw, mae'n ffaith
fod pendefigiaeth marwnadu blin
ar ben, a'r werin ar waith.

Don't you smile?
Emyr Lewis, 1957 –

The wind and rain have been and gone,
the stars are back in shoal,
and Ab Yr Ynad's had a shock:–
grief's turned to rock 'n roll.

All the men who once were fools
have now turned much the wiser;
the land and sea are back in place
and are displaced no longer.

At last the noise of clashing oaks
has stopped, and it's a fact
that elegies no longer reign
now that the people act.

Dewi Bebb

Ynom oll mae cof am ŵr
a gollwyd, yr asgellwr
dewr ei wedd a chwim ei droed
a wibiodd drwy ein maboed
i roi'r bêl yng nghorneli
ein breuddwydion eon ni.

Hyd feysydd lleidiog hogyn,
yn ei goch, mewn du a gwyn,
fel silowét dôi eto
i sgori cais caeau'r co',
yntau'n croesi, a ni'n iau,
y lein yn ein calonnau.

Mae hen wae am un a aeth
ar elor dwy farwolaeth;
ddwywaith gwaeth yw'n hiraeth ni
a'n doeau'n un â Dewi.
Collwyd ef, collwyd hefyd
gyfrinach ryw burach byd.

Dewi Bebb
Idris Reynolds, 1942 –

All of us hold in memory
a man who's missed, the winger, he
who quick of foot and slow to yield
sprinted through our boyhood fields,
planting the rugby ball with ease
in corners of our fantasies.

Through our muddy fields he sped
in black and white, in Wales' red,
like a silhouette, to score
tries in the memory once more;
thereby crossing, by his darts,
the line drawn in our youthful hearts.

We doubly mourn the fields of praise
that brightened up our yesterdays
in emptiness of heart and mind
two different deaths were intertwined,
in Dewi's wake, as time did tell,
a younger world was lost as well.

Dewi Bebb (1938 – 1996) was an outstanding Welsh rugby player, a fast try machine on the wing.

Darllen ei grys

(Ymadrodd milwyr Awstralia am weithred hel
llau o'u dillad yn y ffosydd)

Clec ar ôl clec yn nhawelwch y ffos;
mae Owen John yn darllen ei grys.
Plyga'i ben dros destun sy'n ei ysu'n fyw
a'i 'winedd yn clecian ac yn ysgwyd
llythyren 'rôl llythyren goch o'r wlanen;

cadfridog diwyd y difa distaw,
mor ddistaw fel y clywo'i hun yn llyncu'n sych,
megis cyn datod botymau cynta cariad
a diffodd gwrthsafiad â ffrwydrad gwefusau
– bu llun hon yn gynnes dan ei grys...

A manion fel'na sy'n ei sadio:
cusan rasal; gweld ei hun mewn llygad o ddrych...
Nes gwisgo ohono ei grys drachefn
a diflannu,
i wead map ar fwrdd pencadlys,
i slaes pensil o ymosodiad coch
a chadfridog arall yn chwythu
naddion ei finiwr o blygion ei fap.

Clec ar ôl clec yn nhawelwch y ffos...

Reading his shirt

(Australian soliders' term for the act of delousing
their clothes in the trenches)
Ifor ap Glyn, 1961 –

Crack after crack in the quiet of the trench;
Owen John is reading his shirt.
Head bent to a text that eats him alive
his fingernails cracking and shaking
letter after red letter from the flannel;

the busy general of the silent slaughter,
so silent that he hears his own dry gulping,
as before undoing the first buttons of love
and annihilating resistance with a labial explosion
– her photo was warm under his shirt...

And it's details like that which steady him:
a razor's kiss; beholding himself in a mirror's eye...
Until he puts on his shirt again
and disappears,
into the fabric of a map on an HQ table,
into the pencil slash of a scarlet attack
and another general blowing
his pencil shavings from the folds of his map.

Crack after crack in the quiet of the trench...

A470

'Ydyn ni yna eto?'

Llond sedd gefn o gegau
bacon rolls a quavers
a ribena
yn hala'r car i ddawnsio
hyd odre
Cadair Idris.

Cyfri amser mewn niwl
i fetronom y weipars
amyneddgar.

'Pam fod y gogledd mor bell?'

Hir pob aros
i'r rhai sydd
wedi'u dal
yn ein hunfan
gan blant.

Yn y drych fe gawsom
gip
ar ein gilydd
a gwenu.

A470
Mari George, 1973 –

'Are we there yet?'

A back-seat-full
of bacon rolls and quavers
and ribena mouths
setting the car dancing
at the foot
of Cadair Idris.

Marking time in a mist
to the metronome of the patient
wipers.

'Why is the north so far?'

Every wait's a long wait
for those of us
stuck
with children.

In the mirror we caught
a glimpse
of each other
and smiled.

Fel hyn, mae'n siŵr

Fel hyn, mae'n siŵr, yr oedd yr hafau gynt:
yr allt yn bistyll haul, a thonnau Enlli
ac oglau gwin a genod ar y gwynt
a chwrw hallt yn setlo'n sŵn yr heli.
Mae'n flêr ar ddec y dafarn, rhai ar stolion
yn gwegian; mae 'na rai yn swatio'n nes;
mae pennau'n llenwi hefo mabinogion
a'r sêr yn syllu i'r tywod wedi'r gwres.
Mi faglwn fyny'r rhiw yn ôl i'n gwersyll,
i'n sachau cysgu; chwyrnu ben wrth droed.
Llŷn ŵyr, pan ddaw hi'n adeg tynnu'r pebyll
na fydd ar ôl, bnawn fory, fel erioed
ond patshyn crin o wair, stwmp ambell ffag,
a phob un drosto'i hun yn pacio'i fag.

This, I'm sure
Rhys Iorwerth, 1983 –

This, I'm sure, is how the summers were:
the slope awash with sun, and Bardsey rollers
and scents of wine and girls still in the air
and salt beer settling to the sound of breakers.
In the pub, it's all at sea, some sagging
on their stools, and some are huddling closer;
heads are aswim with tales, and stars are staring
down at the sands, now that the heat is over.
Then back to camp we'll stumble up the hill
where in sleeping bags, head to foot, we'll snore
and by the time the tents are struck, there will
be left, but as of old (Llŷn knows), no more
than a shrivelled patch of grass, and stumps of fags,
and each man for himself, packing his bags.

Oriau mân

Mae pefrio'r sêr wedi'r diwrnod oer
o gylch y bae
yn goron ar y cyfan,
a tho hir ein Senedd
yn dafod,
am lyfu'n awchus
o donnau du'r môr, ac o dramor
gan lowcio ryw hyder tawel.

Hyder, nid fel ton
ond yn llif cyson
fel nant y mynydd,
a'i diferion tawel
yn llifo,
heb sŵn hyd yn oed.

Mae tafod to'r Senedd
yn sychedig am hynny.
Nid am heip
ac nid am ein hawr fawr,
ond am hyder ein horiau bychain,
di-nod.

The small hours
Catrin Dafydd, 1982 –

A crown of stars glitters
over the bay
after the chilly day,
and our Senedd's long roof
a tongue,
eager to lap
from the sea's black waves, and beyond,
gulping a quiet confidence.

Confidence, not like a wave
but a constant flow
like the mountain stream
flowing,
without even a sound.

The tongue of the Senedd's roof
thirsts for that.
Not for hype
and not for our hour of glory,
but for the confidence of our small, insignificant
hours.

The Senedd (parliament house), Cardiff

Mwy na thân mewn eithinen

Maddau, Gwen, faint fy ngweniaith,
maddau im wehyddu iaith
yn dynn, dynn o'th gwmpas di,
maddau im orfod meddwi
ar win fy ngeiriau o hyd
a phrofi'r cyffur hefyd;
maddau mor fas fy nhraserch,
maddau gusanau fy serch
yng ngodre'r sêr; maddau siom
yr un nos a ranasom.

Roedd golau holl sylltau'r sêr
yn gudynnog o dyner
yn dy wallt, a'th lygaid di'n
dawel fel lleuad ewin.
Yfais o gawg dy wefus
gan brofi holl lesni'r llus;
ffoli'n llwyr ar dy ddwyrudd,
troi'n geiban ar gusan gudd
wrth hel mwyar ola'r haf
o'u rhigolau dirgelaf.

Forgive, Gwen
Gruffudd Antur, 1992 –

Forgive, Gwen, my flattery,
forgive my weaving words tightly
about you, and that I should be
ever of a tendency
to drink my words like wine unto
excess, and get high on them too.
Forgive my passion's shallowness,
my love's kisses and caresses
under the stars, that night we spent:
forgive the disillusionment.

All the starlight silvery
shone curling, curling tenderly
in your hair, your eyes quiescent
as the silent new moon's crescent.
From the goblet of your lip
I blue of blueberries did sip;
by your cheeks infatuated,
by hidden kiss, intoxicated,
gathering, from hidden crannies
the last of summer's luscious berries.

Profais win dy gyfrinach
nes aeth hud y funud fach
yn oer, a'n diodydd ni'n
gynrhonog gan hen rawnwin
afiach, a chyfeddach fwyn
yr hen win yn troi'n wenwyn.
Ie, maddau imi waddod
y rhyfyg a fu, gan fod
i wynfyd serch ofid sy'n
ei wneud yn uffern wedyn.

Fe ddaw'r heulwen drwy'r llenni'n
siswrn drwy ein neithiwr ni;
rwyf yn oer; wyf un na wêl
y wawr sy'n goch ar orwel;
y gorwel lle daw'n geiriau
ynghyd i wahanu dau.
Nid yw haul diwrnod o haf
yn malio, ac mi welaf
waddod cyfamod a fu
yn nhawelwch dy wely.

Of your secret, for a moment,
I drank deep: then its enchantment
grew cold, and our drink took on
the taint of grapes in rot far gone,
and vintage wine's sweet company
had soured unto toxicity.
Forgive presumption's dregs in me.
for love, however heavenly
contains within itself, as well,
a grief that makes of heaven, hell.

Through the blinds comes the sun's light
slashing through our previous night;
I'm cold, I'm one who cannot see
dawn's red horizon before me;
that line where our words congregate
to render us both separate.
The summer sun climbs heedlessly
into the morning, and I see
the dregs of a commitment spread
in the silence of your bed.

Maddau, Gwen, fy nghân heno,
maddau'r serch a maddau'r siom.
Tafla f'awen, Gwen, dros go',
maddau bob gair o'm heiddo.
Er mor ffôl yw bodoli
os na chaf fod hefo ti,
mi wn, er bod undod dau
yn oer, fe fydd 'na eiriau
rhyngom tra pery'r angen
am eiliad o'th gariad, Gwen.

Forgive, Gwen, my song to you,
the love and disappointment too.
Cast, Gwen, all my muse away,
forgive me every word I say.
Though to exist is lunacy
unless I can have you with me,
I know, however cold may grow
the bond that held us, words will flow
between us, Gwen, whilst in my core
I need your love one second more.